CRIMES OF WAR

ROGER HUTCHINSON

CRIMES OF WAR
THE ANTANAS GECAS AFFAIR

MAINSTREAM
PUBLISHING PROJECTS

Copyright © Roger Hutchinson, 1994

The moral right of the author has been asserted

First published in Great Britain in 1994 by
MAINSTREAM PUBLISHING PROJECTS
Edinburgh

ISBN 1 85158 612 1

A catalogue record for this book is available from
the British Library

Typeset in Palatino by CentraCet Limited, Cambridge,
Printed and bound in Great Britain by Mackays of Chatham PLC

There is no hope that the boundless horror of Nazi Germany can be transmitted entire to the generations that will succeed us. There is a limit to what we can absorb of other people's experience. There is also a limit to how guilty we should feel about being unable to remember. Santayana was probably wrong when he said that those who forget the past are condemned to relive it. Those who remember are condemned to relive it too. Besides, freedoms are not guaranteed by historians and philosophers, but by a broad consent among the common people about what constitutes decent behaviour. Decency means nothing if it is not vulgarised. Nor can the truth be passed on without being simplified. The most we can hope for is that it shall not be travestied.

Clive James, television critic, the *Observer*,
10 September 1978.

1

It was observed with the Jews that they often leave their
residences in the flat country, probably emigrating towards the
south, attempting to evade the operations initiated against
them. Since they are still making common cause with the
communists and partisans, the total elimination of this element
alien to the nation is being undertaken. The operations carried
out toward this end have so far taken place in the east section
of the area, in the old Soviet Russian border area and along the
railway line Minsk–Brest–Litovsk. In addition, in the area of the
Commandant in Byelorussia, the Jews are being collected in the
flat country in ghettos of larger municipalities . . . During a
purge in the area Slutsk–Kleck by the reserve police unit 11,
5,900 Jews were shot to death.

> Monthly Report from 11 October–10 November 1941,
> Wehrmacht Commander, Ostland.

The heavy lorries of the two German companies of Order
Police and their Lithuanian auxiliary battalion rolled into Slutsk
at first light on 27 October 1941. It was three weeks to the day
since the Lithuanians had left their native barracks for the
sprawling eastlands of Byelorussia – White Russia, or White
Ruthenia, as the Germans had rechristened their newly con-
quered territory – and they were, by then, becoming familiar
with their duties there.

Those duties had little in common with the stirring orders
which had been issued to them earlier in the month, back in

Lithuania. 'The reconstruction of Europe,' they had been told on 4 October, 'will take place under the leadership of the Great Reich's Leader after the greatest enemy of all humanity – Bolshevism – is exterminated; and that the nations of Europe will be rewarded with standing in Europe according to merits which they will earn in current battle going on under the leadership of the Great Leader Adolf Hitler . . . We have to continue contributing as much as we can to the final extermination of Bolshevism which threatened all of cultured Europe.'

'Soldiers,' the address had concluded, 'as you depart, fulfil your missions with resolute will, honesty and with honour. Always and everywhere show yourselves worthy of the noble name of a Lithuanian soldier, because you are the representatives of the entire Lithuanian nation.' The 400 volunteer auxiliaries were then told that they would depart at 0500 hours on 6 October 1941, for the Minsk, Borosov and Slutsk areas of Byelorussia 'to clean these areas of the remnants of the Bolshevik army and Bolshevik partisans'.

At 8.00 a.m. on 27 October a German 1st lieutenant of Order Police Battalion 11 appeared in the office of the German governor of Slutsk, Gebietskommissar Carl. The 1st lieutenant identified himself as an adjutant to Major Franz Lechthaler, who was presently on the outskirts of Slutsk with a force of German and Lithuanian companies.

The 1st lieutenant's next comments caused some alarm to Gebietskommissar Carl. Major Lechthaler's orders, he said, were to liquidate all of the Jews in the city of Slutsk. The four companies had 48 hours in which to complete this task. Carl, an aging Nazi Party member of some standing who had been given the sultanate of Slutsk in acknowledgment of past loyalty to the cause, was visibly shaken. Slutsk had a population of 15,000 people, of whom no fewer than 8,000 were Jewish, many of them engaged in vital local industries.

Gebietskommissar Carl had not assumed the government of Slutsk in order to preside over the destruction of its civilian workforce, and he protested. He had no notice of this action, he expostulated . . . he must in any case discuss it with the commander.

By 8.30 a.m. Lechthaler and his companies had arrived in Slutsk. Carl took his objections directly to the major. This action was impossible, he insisted, as all the Jews had been sent to work, and to start murdering them would cause frightful confusion. There must be prior preparation. At the least, Lechthaler was obliged to give Carl a day's notice. Could he not postpone his activities for 24 hours? Lechthaler shook his head. He had actions to pursue throughout the region, and only two days were available for Slutsk. By the morning of 29 October, Slutsk must be absolutely free of Jews. Carl was appalled. There could not be an arbitrary liquidation of Jews in Slutsk, he insisted. Most of them were craftsmen, and indispensable to the local economy. All vital enterprises would instantly be paralysed if the Jews were killed. Lechthaler seemed to relent. He agreed that Jews currently occupied in workshops – and carrying identifying papers to that effect – would not be disturbed, and that their families would be sorted and spared by two of Carl's officials. Lechthaler, a diffident, 52-year-old former policeman with First World War experience of the Soviet Union and a reputed distaste for Adolf Hitler, convinced the nervous Gebietskommissar that his liquidations would be selective. 'The commander in no way opposed my position,' Carl would write later, 'so in good faith I believed that the action would therefore be carried out accordingly.'

Within hours a frantic Carl was on the telephone to his superior in the regional headquarters at Minsk, General Commissioner Wilhelm Kube. Horrifying atrocities are being committed here, he wailed. Major Lechthaler has broken his word. All Jews, without exception, were being taken from factories and workshops, marched to the outskirts of Slutsk, and summarily shot. Carl found himself hurrying through the ghetto, grasping wildly at Jews of recognisable economic value and dragging them with his own hands out of the stumbling queues of the condemned. By noon, the workshops were already closing through panic and undermanning.

Major Franz Lechthaler had already departed from Slutsk, heading for other fields. Carl eventually found his deputy, a German captain, and furiously insisted that the action be halted at once. The captain shrugged him off. His orders from Lechthaler, he said, were to 'make the city free of Jews without exception', as they had already done in other cities. This 'cleansing', the captain informed Carl, was proceeding on political grounds, and nowhere had economic factors so far played a role. He nonetheless agreed to halt the murder until that evening.

Carl had time enough only to take stock. Within hours the holocaust had ignited again. 'The city itself offered a horrible picture,' recalled Carl. 'With indescribable brutality, by the German policemen as well but especially by the Lithuanians, the Jews and also White Russians were taken out of their lodgings and driven together. There was shooting everywhere in the city, and in the individual streets bodies of Jews who had been shot were piled up. The White Russians had the greatest difficulty in extricating themselves from the round-up . . .'

Men, women and children were beaten senseless with truncheons or shot as they ran. Lithuanian auxiliaries drove Carl's own officers from the streets with their careless gunplay, and proceeded to plunder, maim and murder. Watches and rings were torn from the arms and fingers of young women; leather, textiles and gold were appropriated from the workshops. Jewish girls were sent racing frantically around Slutsk in search of the 5,000 roubles which, they were evilly and mendaciously assured, would ransom their parents' lives. Carl could not bring himself to visit the official killing grounds on the border marches of Slutsk, but there, he was assured, truly terrible things had happened. Not all of those shot had been killed. Some of them had crawled from the mass graves and made their ghastly way, naked, soiled and bloody, back into the outlying streets, like so many Lazaruses: a nightmarish contingent of the undead.

Wilhelm Kube listened to Gebietskommissar Carl's despairing telephone call, and instructed him to put his complaint in writing. Carl did this three days later, immediately after the Order Police had left Slutsk and followed their commander, Franz Lechthaler, to Baranovichi. 'I now ask only that one request be granted me,' concluded the civil governor of Slutsk to his superior in Minsk. 'In the future, spare me without fail from this police battalion.'

Sixty miles south of the Byelorussian capital, Minsk, and a mere 150 miles from the Polish border, Slutsk had been one of the first communities to fall to the Nazi invasion of the Soviet Union. The German blitzkrieg reached this modest township on the northern edge of the Pripyat marshes within days of its incursion. Operation Barbarossa, the violent breach of the Soviet–German pact which would finally cost Hitler his war and untold millions their lives, was launched on 22 June 1941. By the end of that month, Slutsk and all of its surrounds were in the civil and military control of the Third Reich.

Gebietskommissar Carl was given a humble charge when he was given the governorship of Slutsk. His responsibilities, as he read them, lay in directing the light industries and agricultural base of the area – the tanneries, cart-builders, metalworkshops, smithies, and cabinet-makers – to labour for the Reichstag. In his itinerary the large and industrious Jewish community of Slutsk – whose ghetto dominated the centre of the town, whose smaller communities speckled the windswept countryside, whose Yiddish tongue was everywhere to be heard and whose ancient, vibrant Central European culture was everywhere to be seen – was vital. Without it, he would command the husk of a town.

The Jews of Slutsk were, of course, immediately subjected to the everyday degradations of Jews elsewhere in the Third Reich. They were commanded, man, woman, and child, to wear on their left breast the yellow Mogen David, the Star of

David, measuring eight by ten centimetres. They were forbidden from walking on the pavements of Slutsk. They were
denied provisions from the government's foodstores. Their
labour for the Reich was unpaid. Those not in regular profitable
work had to report each morning to the civil authority of
Gebietskommissar Carl, where they would be herded with
rifle-butts to menial, gutter-sweeping, rubble-clearing tasks
about the town. In what waking hours they were spared, they
had to scavenge for food and fuel.

But they were alive. By the June of 1941 Jews throughout
occupied Europe had been ritually dispossessed, beaten and
starved. They had seen their synagogues torched and their
shops plundered and their businesses destroyed. They had
been forced into the illusory safety of exile in neighbouring
countries. They had been raped and murdered, singly and
collectively, in random, brutal attacks, and they had been
killed in gratuitous reprisals for resistance activities, real or
imagined. They had been dehumanised by Nazi propaganda
in which they were portrayed on posters and in film as vermin
and as demons.

Yet by the June of 1941 no Jewish community in Europe
had seen more than three percent of its people cold-bloodedly
murdered. Frightened, subjugated, defiled, lost and hungry
they might be; but the Jews of Europe were still alive. And, as
a whole, they counted themselves more likely than not to stay
alive. In the June of 1941 the persecution which they had
suffered for almost a decade in some areas of the Reich seemed
still to be identifiable, to be located in their folk-memory as
another long and vicious pogrom which would come, and go,
and leave its victims – the Jewish nation in Europe – bowed
but unbroken; wounded and reduced, but alive. They still, in
the June of 1941, clung to the hope that the Third Reich was
possessed only by the simple temporary insanity of a pogrom.
They had only, at that time, been licked by the young flames
of the holocaust.

Rochelle Weissman was 15 years old on 27 October 1941.

Born in Kamen Kashirskiy, 150 miles away in the north-western Ukraine, her family had moved to Slutsk when Rochelle was an infant. Her mother died when she was eight years old, and until her father remarried she raised her three younger sisters while pursuing her own education. She was finishing her eighth year at the public school in Slutsk when the Germans arrived at the end of June 1941, and all education for Jewish children was ended.

Her father was killed shortly after the first German advance on Slutsk. He had worked in a pickling factory, and when he heard that the factory was in flames but that much of its produce was salvable, he felt it his duty to go and investigate. The Germans found him, and Rochelle Weissman never saw her father again. She at first joined the work details in daytime, clearing the bricks of burned-out buildings from the streets of Slutsk, urged on by a German overseer's whip, and scavenged for scorched, abandoned bread in those same buildings at night. After two weeks she found a job as a cleaner in a large restaurant that the occupying German troops had built out of a state department store.

For three months Rochelle Weissman worked in the restaurant; cleaning tables after German soldiers, scrubbing floors, fetching wood from forced Jewish labourers to keep the large ovens burning, taking home discarded rolls of bread and soup to supplement the corn and potatoes which her step-mother, her sisters and her half-brother were able to take from the fields.

When Major Franz Lechthaler and his four companies of Order Police and Lithuanian auxiliaries arrived in Slutsk and commenced work on the morning of 27 October 1941, Rochelle Weissman was working in the restaurant. At about 10.00 a.m. she heard disturbances and rifle-fire in the street, and looked outside. There she saw groups of people being harried along the road by soldiers wearing an unfamiliar uniform. By October, Rochelle Weissman was familiar with the dark green battledress of a German soldier, and the uniform of these

soliders was lighter, much lighter: it was leaf-green, the colour
of a field of new grass. And they spoke to each other in a
language which she did not understand. Some of their prey
attempted to escape from these soldiers, and as they did so
they were shot dead. Others were beaten viciously into line;
and all of the time trucks drew up and disgorged more soldiers
in light green uniforms.

As if in a trance, Rochelle Weissman moved outside.
Approaching her, down the street, she saw her three young
sisters surrounded by five or six soldiers. The youngest, an
eight-year-old, broke away from the group and started to run
to Rochelle. The girl was seized by one of the soldiers, a big
man of about 25 years, who beat her furiously until she fell,
screaming, to the ground. Rochelle was held and forcibly
restrained by another woman, a Gentile workmate from the
restaurant, and when she was able to look up again, her sisters
had gone. 'Suddenly,' she would say later, 'I saw nothing
there.'

From all corners the streets filled up with files of panicked
humanity, groups of 50, groups of a hundred, being beaten on
their way. And everywhere that Rochelle Weissman looked,
people were being killed. Men fled to the rooftops, where they
were picked off like birds by sniping soldiers, and dead bodies
littered the roads and the forbidden pavements of Slutsk.

Rochelle's Russian workmate pulled her back into the
restaurant and through the building, out of the back doors and
in through the side entrance of an adjoining government
bookstore. There was an empty barrel standing in the bookstore, and the Russian girl urged Rochelle Weissman and
another, Jewish, friend inside it. Then she took books from the
surrounding shelves and piled them on top of the two girls
until they were entirely covered. She told them to stay there
until she returned with further news.

For the remainder of that day and all the following night
Rochelle and the other girl stayed in the barrel. They heard the
gunfire and the screams, usually muffled and at a distance,

but once they heard a recognisable voice. It was that of a young Jewish boy who worked chopping wood for the restaurant's ovens. They heard him protest, and they heard him run to the roof of their building. They heard soldiers talking in that unfamiliar language, and then they heard the shots, and the final truncated shriek of the boy as he fell.

Between ten and 11 o'clock the next morning their Gentile friend returned. 'It's quiet now,' she said. 'You can go out.' They left the building and saw the body of the young wood-cutter lying in the street. Cold and terrified, Rochelle Weissman wandered through the apocalyptic thoroughfares of Slutsk until she came to the town barracks. There were hordes of people – Jewish people, she instantly recognised – sitting and lying on the ground, entirely surrounded by soldiers. As she watched they were loaded piecemeal on to the backs of trucks and driven sharply away, with a soldier standing at each corner of the tumbril. If a passenger screamed, or attempted to jump clear, they were instantly shot.

Rochelle returned to the restaurant and pleaded with her workmates for help, help of any kind. There were German women working there and she begged them to go to the barracks and find her family. She wept and she gave them gifts, but they offered no response. 'They listened to me,' she recalled in old age, 'they heard, they talked among themselves.'

All of that second day and all of that night the trucks and their human cargo trundled through the streets of Slutsk. Some of the cargo, she heard, had escaped, and been assisted by Russian civilians, but very few evaded the rifles of the guards. Rochelle Weissman spent a night alone in her family's home, and then realised that she would never again see her three sisters and her half-brother. When she emerged, and the battalions of Order Police had departed from Slutsk, a guarded and board-wired ghetto was being created for the 25 per cent of the town's Jews who had survived – the few essential workers that Gebietskommissar Carl had managed to rescue.

Rochelle avoided that ghetto. She slept outside it, in the house of a friendly Russian woman, or in the toilets of the restaurant. She did not wear the Mogen David. She found herself the clothing of a Gentile from the villages: a kerchief, boots, and coat; and in the spring of 1942 she passed a medical test which asserted that she was both fit and a Gentile, and Rochelle Weissman was assigned to a work detail far from Byelorussia, in the capital of the Reich itself: Berlin. When that city fell to the Allied advance in May 1945, and was divided between the powers, she found herself to be living in the American Zone. She applied for a displaced person's entry to the United States, and was granted citizenship.

By that time Rochelle knew what language those strange soldiers in light green uniforms had been talking to each other. Many people had told her, on several different occasions, that it was Lithuanian.

Juozas Janos Aleksynas would remember Slutsk in later years as one of the bloodiest massacres of civilians performed in the occupied Soviet Union by his Lithuanian battalion. Aleksynas had joined up as a 26-year-old, immediately after the German occupation of Lithuania, in July 1941. He had recently been discharged from his compulsory service in the Lithuanian Army, and was attracted to the 2nd Company of Lithuanian auxiliaries on the triple grounds of sympathy with the Nazi scourge of Bolshevism, a fondness of the notion of keeping 'order' in Lithuania, and a belief that his service would be required only for six months. He had been a corporal in the Lithuanian Army, and he retained that rank as a volunteer for the Third Reich.

So it was that Juozas Aleksynas became one of the Lithuanians who drove south-eastward out of Kaunas barracks in the October of 1941, with their commander's exhortation to show themselves 'worthy of the noble name of a Lithuanian soldier' ringing in their ears, south-eastward to Byelorussia, to Minsk, to Borosov, and to Slutsk.

They travelled in covered lorries to their new barracks at

Minsk. From there they were despatched to the towns and villages of central Byelorussia to pursue their actions. Soviet prisoners-of-war would usually have preceded them to the venue, and dug large pits on the outskirts of the town.

The pits were already dug when Aleksynas and his colleagues arrived at Slutsk. There were so many pits that he could not count them, littered around the marshy fields, each one a metre-and-a-half in depth and up to 30 metres long. 'We had herded the Jews from the ghettos in Slutsk,' a 77-year-old Juozas Aleksynas would later tell, sitting in his squalid cottage in rural Lithuania, 'going to their homes and herding them into the square, marching them out.

'The whole thing lasted two days. Everyone was taken: men, women, children, old, young and they were all Jews. They were made to march to the place of execution. We were careful. The young men were not allowed to get together in case they caused trouble. They were mixed with the old, and people who had difficulty walking, or with the very young. Mothers carried children. They did not give us any trouble. They were silent, and resigned.'

These prayerful, dignified victims were made to lie face down in the bottom of the pits, and there they were shot by Lithuanian soldiers, on the orders of Lithuanian officers, with a rifle whose fixed bayonet was placed at the nape of the neck. Then Corporal Aleksynas and his fellows would retire, splattered with blood and brains and bone, to the trees to suck upon cigarettes and anticipate the 100 grams of vodka that would shortly come their way, while their officers moved among the dead and dying.

'These were not partisans who were being killed,' Aleksynas would later attest. 'They were Jews. It was clear that our purpose in the Minsk area, although it had never been expressed as such, was the mass killing and extermination of Jewish people.

'Throughout all of these mass killings, the Germans were not involved in the shooting of Jews. They would surround

the area and then send us, the Lithuanians, in . . . the killings
were always carried out by Lithuanians or Latvians. The
Germans would often photograph us doing it. The only
involvement the Germans would have would be with the
officers in assisting the Lithuanian officers, and finishing off
any survivors.'

Fifty-one years later, in 1992, the 77-year-old Juozas Aleksynas still clearly remembered his superior officers. His platoon
commander had joined the battalion only as it left Lithuania.
He was not an easy man to forget. He was tall and young and
handsome, with an athletic build, chestnut-coloured hair, and
an engaging manner. Distinctively, he wore the dark blue
uniform of the former Lithuanian Air Force, and he held the
rank of lieutenant.

He was fluent in German, this Lithuanian platoon commander, and as the convoy moved into Byelorussia he travelled
at its head, with the officers of the German Order Police. He
would stand in the company of German officers in the towns
and in the killing fields; he would issue orders through his
sergeants to allocate shooting parties, to shoulder arms, and to
fire. In this murderous arena, these backwood fires which
marked the beginning of a terrible holocaust, Juozas Aleksynas
would recall that his platoon commander was 'everywhere'.

No, he was not an easy man for Aleksynas to forget. His
name was Gecevicius. Antanas Gecevicius.

2

On a cold Thursday morning in Glasgow at the end of October 1986, senior investigative journalist Bob Tomlinson sat in Scottish Television's daily news conference, and waited to be called.

It was a news conference like many another: a 'lazy' day for stories; a day when obviously nothing was going to happen. Twenty or 30 journalists sat about, having scoured the morning's papers, scratching their heads. There were industrial redundancies, the odd murderous attack in Glasgow . . . Tomlinson found himself drifting away, only half-listening to his colleagues. His position at the table meant that he would be one of the last to speak, and as his thoughts wandered he looked down occasionally at the small newspaper cutting in his hand. It was taken from that morning's edition of the Scottish tabloid *Daily Record*. It read:

> Premier Margaret Thatcher was told last night that at least 17 Nazi war criminals are living in Britain under false names.
>
> And one of the wanted men is believed to be in Edinburgh, after fleeing from Lithuania, where he allegedly helped to murder thousands of Jews.
>
> The Simon Weisenthal Centre in Los Angeles yesterday handed over the list to Britain's Californian Consul-General, Donald Ballantyne.
>
> And Rabbi Hier, who compiled the dossier, said: 'We have every confidence the British government will act in this matter.
>
> 'It's the first time such a list has been presented to Britain.'

The dossier was compiled after the Weisenthal Centre gained access to immigration documents on people who fled from Lithuania and Latvia after the war.

Last month, a list of 40 names and alleged crimes was given to the government of Australia.

Tomlinson held on to the clipping like a talisman. He found it impossible to believe. It was 40 years out of date, and in any event it could not be true. We don't have war criminals living in Great Britain, he told himself, and we certainly don't have them living in Scotland. Australia, maybe, but Edinburgh! . . . He looked at the clipping again, as the conference droned around towards him. It was a slow day for news . . .

The conference chairman, Eric Wilkie, a producer of the old school of journalism, a man who believed in giving his journalists rope, took the meeting gradually round the table. Normally Tomlinson would not have been so shy about coming forward. Normally he would have spoken earlier. But normally he had something to offer. That day, he had nothing. Almost nothing.

'Bob?'

Wilkie was looking at him.

'You haven't said much.'

Tomlinson looked down again at his preposterous clipping. 'I'm really a bit lost here,' he offered. 'There's a story in the *Record* that I just find incredible. Apparently there's an alleged war criminal living in Edinburgh.'

'What is it?'

Tomlinson took a breath. It sounded absurd. 'The Weisenthal Centre,' he said, 'has handed a list to the British Consulate in Los Angeles. A list of 17 Nazi war criminals. I don't know.' He looked at Wilkie. 'There's something not right,' he said, 'there's something ringing bells. It seems to me, they've either got it dead wrong or they've got it dead right.'

Wilkie shrugged. 'Okay,' he said. 'Run with it and let

me know how it goes. Just follow it through – until it falls down.'

Sitting at his desk, Tomlinson wondered who to call in order to deflate this fanciful story. He felt slightly foolish, as if he was chasing a flier that was bound to end up in the bin. He hated the idea of wasting time. The bulky figure of David Scott, then Scottish Television's head of news and current affairs, wandered through the newsroom asking what was in the queue. Scott and Tomlinson had worked together before, on a Sunday newspaper's investigative unit, and they knew well each other's qualities.

'Have they named him?' asked Scott.

'No,' said Tomlinson. 'No, they haven't.'

Who to call? he thought. Where on earth do I start? He got the number of the Weisenthal Centre in Los Angeles from International Inquiries, and then pulled his hand away from the telephone. It would be the middle of the night in LA. Who else would know about these things? The Holocaust Centre! Yad Vashem, the Holocaust Centre in Israel. They'd be awake.

Tomlinson telephoned Jerusalem. Inexplicably, his call was answered by a man named Ephraim Zuroff, who was – Tomlinson would soon learn to his amazement – the Simon Weisenthal Centre's agent in Israel. In all of that vast building, with all of those telephones, Bob Tomlinson's call was answered by Ephraim Zuroff. The bells were ringing louder.

Zuroff, a small, hard man from the Bronx who had lost some of his family to the Order Police and their local auxiliary units in Byelorussia, who was as deeply involved as anybody, anywhere in the world in the quest to bring Nazi war criminals to justice, listened carefully to Tomlinson's request for telephone numbers and for help.

'The man you want to speak to,' said Zuroff finally, 'is Eli Rosenbaum.'

'Who's he?'

'Eli Rosenbaum is a Manhattan attorney, a young firebrand of a lawyer. He is also the senior counsel to the World Jewish Congress in New York. Call Rosenbaum.'

As he dialled New York, Bob Tomlinson felt the beginning of a familiar thrill. There was, perhaps, something going on here. It may not be just a publicity stunt by the Weisenthal Centre. There could be a story . . . He was put straight through to Eli Rosenbaum, and he read out the clipping from the *Daily Record*. 'What's his name?' asked Tomlinson.

'Gecas,' Rosenbaum replied firmly. 'Antony Gecas. Also known as Antanas Gecevicius.'

'How do you know?'

'Because I have his file. I worked for a while with the Office of Special Investigations at the United States Department of Justice, and I have the Gecas file. But that doesn't matter. You asked for the name and I've given you the name. What are you going to do?'

'I want to do a story.'

Rosenbaum. paused. 'If you're going to do a story, you must realise what you're getting into,' he said slowly.

'It's just a story.'

'No, no. You don't know the half of it. You are only touching the tip of the iceberg. You do not know what you are getting into here.'

'Tell me what I'm getting into.'

'There has been a cover-up,' said Rosenbaum. 'A gigantic cover-up.'

Bob Tomlinson sighed. 'You hear this all the time,' he said.

'This is something much bigger than you realise,' said Rosenbaum patiently. 'I am going to fax you two items. If you want the remainder, which I have, you will not get it by post, or by fax. I will bring it to you or you will come here.'

'Fine,' said Tomlinson. 'Fax me the items.'

Bob Tomlinson had arrived late at journalism. He was, in 1986, 43 years old, a fit man with a consuming love of sport and a fondness for wearing running shoes beneath his well-cut suits and bright ties. Until the age of 29 he had worked as an office-manager and an accountant: an apprenticeship which, he remained convinced, served him well. He had led a life outside the newsroom.

In 1971, at the age of 29, he had taken his first job in journalism, with the *Sunday Post*. He had moved from there to the Glasgow *Evening News*, the *Daily Record* and a quality Scottish weekly, since defunct, called the *Sunday Standard*, where he had worked with David Scott. In 1985 he had been named as Scottish Journalist of the Year. In 1986 he followed Scott to Scottish Television, and the move suited well this talkative, energetic man. He won leeway: the ability to pursue or to drop stories as he saw fit; the freedom to move. He was trusted by his producers at Scottish Television not to flog dead horses. It was a trust that he relished.

'I've got his name,' Tomlinson told Eric Wilkie. 'It's Gecas. Antony Gecas. He's in the telephone book – Moston Terrace, Edinburgh. Shall we get an interview?' Tomlinson placed a call to the Edinburgh number. There was no reply.

Early the next day a bundle of papers arrived from Eli Rosenbaum, and Bob Tomlinson studied them with incredulity. There was part of a transcript from a war-crimes trial in the United States. Aside from the accused, one name occurred throughout that transcript. It was the name of Antanas Gecevicius. Tomlinson stopped and read part of it.

Tomlinson picked up another sheaf of paper and turned through its pages with mounting astonishment. It was the copy of an interview which had been conducted in April 1982 by one Neal Sher, deputy director of the United States Justice Department's Office of Special Investigations, the unit established in the United States with a particular brief for investigating war crimes. Sher had travelled to Scotland and taken evidence from Antony Gecas in his Edinburgh home, in the presence of Constable Gordon McBain of Lothian and Borders

Police, in connection with the war-crimes trial of a Jurgis Juodis. Throughout the transcript a careful Sher had got his man to initial key areas of testimony.

Bob Tomlinson studied those three sheets of neatly hand-written paper carefully, steadily, and with a vague sense of wonder. Like early hieroglyphs, the symbols seemed to be charged with a subtext, a deeper meaning waiting to be decoded and given their intended setting, given a purpose:

Edinburgh Scotland
April 16 1982
Antanas Gecas states as follows:

1. I was born on May 26, 1916 in Joukliai, Lithuania. I was known in Lithuania by the name of Antanas Gecevicius.
2. In approximately 1937 I entered the Lithuanian Military Academy in Kaunas. During this training my platoon commander in aviation school was Lieutenant Jurgis Juodis. I know that Jurgis Juodis was in an airplane accident prior to the German occupation of Lithuania.
3. In June 1941 the Germans invaded Lithuania. Shortly thereafter, I joined the Lithuanian forces known as the Second Battalion and called Paqalbinas Policijes Tarnybes Batalionui. The Commander of the Battalion was Major Impulevicius.
4. During the summer of 1941 I was with the Second Battalion in Kaunas. We stayed in Sanciai area barracks.
5. During the time I joined the Second Battalion I saw Jurgis Juodis in his blue Lithuanian Air Force uniform. I believe he was also in the Second Battalion.
6. I remember the following persons as also being in the Second Battalion: Jonas Plunge; Juozas Krikstaponis; Jonas Stunkaitis.
7. In October 1941 the Second Battalion was sent to Minsk; I went with the battalion. We stayed in the Minsk area until approximately 1943. During the period in Minsk we were assigned to cleaning out Russian partisans; I remember going to the Slutsk area to fight.

8. I was shown a photospread of eight pictures. I recognise number eight as looking like Jurgis Juodis and I signed my name to that picture.
9. I have read the above and believe it to be true and accurate.

Three signatures followed: those of Sher and witness McBain, and the tiny, truncated six letters: A Gecas. Did they look nervously scrawled, or was that wishful thinking? Then, a postcript:

10. Shortly after the Second Battalion went to Minsk we went to the village of Dukara. At that time the Jews and suspected communists of Dukara were taken to the forest and shot by members of the Second Battalion; I witnessed this shooting but I did not participate. There were approximately 150 people shot.

Again, the three signatures.
There's all of us fancy journalists around here, breathed Tomlinson to himself, and who knew a thing about this? It's so bizarre, it must be true. A guy from the US government's OSI, one of the most skilled and feared investigative units in the States, comes to Scotland, interviews a Scottish citizen about war crimes in the presence of Lothian and Borders Police, gets a full statement and flies out again – and nobody knew anything about it! Either, thought Tomlinson, we've got it terribly wrong, he just witnessed a few things, as he says, and we're about to throw the whole bag at him . . . or he took part in it.
Or he took part in it.
Tomlinson dialled the Edinburgh number once more, and once more it rang endlessly out. It was a Saturday afternoon. He got hold of Scottish Television's newsroom assistant, Simon Forrest, an experienced fixer for Independent Television News, and arranged to take a film crew to Moston Terrace early on Sunday morning, to doorstep Antony Gecas.
It was a depressing drive along the M8 to Edinburgh on

that Sunday morning. The Scottish Television men had been hoping against hope that they were the only journalists in possession of the identity of the Scot on the Weisenthal Centre's list, but the *Sunday Times* had got there first. They had named him, and actually obtained a couple of brief quotes.

They drove to Moston Terrace and knocked on the door of No. 3. A small Asian woman opened it. Sorry, she said, I am just the housekeeper. But Mr Gecas is not here. He and his family are away for the weekend. Fine, said Tomlinson, we'll be back tomorrow.

Anxious not to waste the time and expense of a television crew, they asked a handful of neighbours what they thought of this strange affair. Most were protective of their fellow resident. Such a perfect gentleman, they said; the ideal neighbour; a quiet, inoffensive man. It was a disgrace that he should be hounded so, that he should be slurred in the *Sunday Times*. You have, Tomlinson was told, no right to pursue him. Only one took a different line. He was an eminent Jewish medical professor, and when the situation was put to him he began to weep. He could not, he said, encompass the horror of the thought.

At 5.00 a.m. on Monday Tomlinson and Forrest left Glasgow again, to rendezvous with an Edinburgh film crew. They sat in cars in Moston Terrace for a long time in that dark, cold dawn, studying Eli Rosenbaum's documents in the glimmer of a pencil torch. At 8.00 a.m. a light went on in the house. Tomlinson wrapped a handful of coins in a handkerchief, put the bundle in his coat pocket, and got out of the car. 'If I'm not out of the house within five minutes,' he told the film crew, 'come in at 10.30.' Then he walked to the front door.

The same woman answered. She looked frightened. Tomlinson introduced himself again. 'Could we see Mr Gecas now, please?' he asked politely. 'I do feel that he should be given the opportunity to put his side of the story.' The woman looked over her shoulder nervously, but this time made no instant denial of his presence, offered no ignorance of his whereabouts, told no white lie about being merely a house-keeper. Suddenly, behind her, Tomlinson saw a human form in the dim light of the hallway. The journalist made an exaggerated shiver, as if he was about to sneeze, pulled the handkerchief out of his pocket, and spilled the coins inside the front door. He stepped forward, apologising, into the house to pick up the money.

In front of him, back-lit by the yellow bulb of a room at the end of the gloomy Victorian hallway, and framed by its open door, stood a large, elderly man dressed in a shirt and trousers. He looked fit and relaxed – so very relaxed, for a man who had been linked with evil in the pages of the *Sunday Times*, and who knew by then that most of the British media was chasing him. He should be under pressure, thought Tomlinson as he looked for the first time at Antanas Gecevi-cius. He should be worried.

Even when everything else had come and gone, after the journeys through the heartlands of the holocaust, after the exposures and the award-winning programmes, after the switches of government policy, the awful, epochal High Court hearings, and the verdict which brought more relief than victory, after all of those things Bob Tomlinson could still not forget and could still only partly understand the quiet, col-lected, premeditated calm of Antanas Gecevicius on that late October morning.

3

The Lithuania into which Antanas Stanislovas was born to Stanislovas and Olimpija Gecevicius on 26 May 1916 was a country about to enjoy its first 20 years of full and undisturbed independence for more than five centuries. In the jigsaw of Central European states, Lithuania had been a readily transferable part since 1386 when the warrior king Jagiello, Vladislav V, took the Grand Duchy of Lithuania – an ancient Slavic property whose enormous ridings stretched from the Baltic to the Black Sea, across steppes, forest and marshland from Konigsberg in the north to Odessa in the south, from the borders of the Holy Roman Empire in the west to the Mongolian Khanate of the Golden Horde in the east – and made it the major part of his kingdom of Poland.

Chipped away by Habsburgs, Russians, and knights of the Teutonic Order over the seething Middle Ages, what remained of Lithuania nonetheless stayed in the Polish Empire throughout its heyday of the fifteenth and sixteenth centuries. It remained Polish when the Peace of Westphalia brought the Thirty Years War to an end in 1648, and it remained Polish throughout the reductions of Jagiello's proud empire by the squeezing forces of East and West in the eighteenth century.

Only in the Second and Third Partitions of Poland in 1793 and 1795 did the greater part of the old Grand Duchy fall into the hands of Imperial Russia – the lands of the Empress Catherine II, Catherine the Great; and its lesser part, the

western forests south of Kovno, ominously into the arms of
the heirs of the Order of Teutonic Knights: the Brandenburg–
Prussian kingdom of Frederick William II.

As the eighteenth century turned into the nineteenth, this
tattered fragment of Baltic land was both Russian and Prussian,
and nothing in the press of mighty ambitions. The collapse of
the Prussians on the heels of Napoleon saw the Russians
extend their sovereignty over the area in 1815, and so Lithuania
remained for 100 years, a nameless entity, unmarked on most
maps, a fragment of colonial booty distinguished only by its
language and a few vain memories.

The First World War restored its sovereignty to what was
left of Lithuania. When the Bolshevik revolution signalled the
effective end of Russian involvement in that conflict in 1917,
the Germans wrung from Moscow the renunciation of any
claim to their Baltic territories at the Treaty of Bresh–Litovsk –
and then, unusually to the poor Lithuanians, their new masters
tossed them the bone of nominal independence. Perhaps
fortunately for this surprised, recently free people, the Germans themselves went under before they could explore the
true dimensions of that 'nominal' independence; and as 1919
came in Lithuania discovered itself to be actually, discernibly
on its own: a separate state within a peaceful Europe, recognised and smiled benignly upon by the League of Nations, that
body which would keep Europe free from war for all time to
come.

When the smoke had cleared, Lithuania, like an innocent
passer-by left clutching the heist after an aborted robbery,
held the greatest prize. She had to forgo her historic town
of Vilna, or Vilnius, which had been taken and held by the
Poles in a defensive action, but half a cake was better than
none, and those who were small children in Lithuania at the
end of the First World War had reason, their parents possibly
told them, for greater optimism than had 30 generations of
their forebears.

The ebb and flow of empires across the great plains of

Central Europe in the preceding centuries had washed its multifarious peoples into all corners. A tiered caste system had emerged, a social stratification which survived well into the twentieth century, even in those vast regions which became republics of the Soviet Union. It followed much the same pattern from the Baltic to the Crimea, and it largely ignored borders. At its head were the remnants of the Polish Empire, the landowners and the titled, Roman Catholic by religion and Polish-speaking. Beneath them lay the 'indigenes' of the region, the smallholders and peasantry who spoke Ukrainian in Byelorussia and Ukraine, and Lithuanian in Lithuania, and whose religion was one of the two main branches of the old Roman Church: Greek Orthodox or Catholic. Next came the 'Volksdeutsch', the ethnic Germans who had spread across the area in the eighteenth century: Protestant, German-speaking farmers whose massive presence in some regions would give Adolf Hitler one of his chief expansionist planks. And last – certainly last, in the eyes of the other three – were the millions of Jews of middle Europe; resident there for centuries, working as pedlars, merchants, and craftsmen, a gregarious people who clustered together in the towns in groups of tightly walled streets known as ghettos, their religion – of course – was the oldest of the great monotheisms, Judaism, and their spoken, sung and written tongue was Yiddish.

Antanas Gecevicius was born into the second of those Lithuanian classes in the small town of Jakuliai. He was brought up to be a devout Roman Catholic. A former school-friend would later remember him as a conscientious but not outstanding student, and certainly not as a bully or even as a leader of other boys. 'He used to say prayers every morning at grammar school.'

Gecevicius left school and joined the Lithuanian Air Force as a cadet. This large, earnest, personable young man applied himself diligently to his work, and was shortly promoted to the rank of junior lieutenant.

That was as far as Antanas Gecevicius would progress in

the Lithuanian Air Force. The outbreak of the Second World War in 1939 squeezed Lithuania, once again, between the mighty ambitions of East and West.

The German–Soviet non-aggression pact was signed while Hitler was planning his invasion of Poland, on 23 August 1939. The forces of the Reich entered Poland eight days later, and on 3 September Great Britain declared war on Germany. The large, public print of the pact between Hitler and Stalin merely insisted that the two powers would not attack each other. A secret protocol attached to it, however, divided Eastern Europe between them. Poland was to be split in two along the River Vistula, which flows through the heart of Warsaw; and Latvia and Estonia were to become part of the Soviet Union, while the third Baltic state, Lithuania, would become a region of greater Germany.

The German Army did not stop at the River Vistula, however. It progressed rapidly eastward at the end of 1939, and the protocol had equally rapidly to be amended. Under the new version the Germans were granted all of eastern Poland up to the River Bug, and the Soviets were allocated Lithuania. On 15 June 1940, the Red Army entered Estonia, Latvia and Lithuania and declared them part of the Soviet Union. It also retook the city of Vilnius from eastern Poland and returned it to the Soviet Socialist Republic of Lithuania.

Communisation progressed apace in the Baltic states: private enterprise was abolished and suspicious bourgeois were rooted out and purged. An estimated 100,000 people were deported to the interior of the Soviet Union from the Baltic states. Many Lithuanians – such as Antanas Gecevicius's older brother – fled the country for the happier grounds of Germany and worked there for the Third Reich. Others formed scattered resistance movements, hiding in the forests, sniping at Soviet occupiers, cursing the Bolsheviks, cursing the Jews who they generally assumed to be hand in glove with the communists and the KGB, and waiting on the day . . .

It was 12 months before the day dawned. As early as

August 1940 Hitler had put in place his plans for Operation Barbarossa: the invasion, conquest and subjugation of the Soviet Union. The vast Russian territories were to become Ostlands of the Reich, with their distant, intractable far-eastern badlands a permanent battleground on the edge of Teutonic civilisation: a perpetual field of war wherein the flower of German manhood could prove and polish its steel for generations to come.

And so on 22 June 1941 German tanks rolled over the borders of their erstwhile ally, taking Joseph Stalin completely by surprise. When, shortly afterwards, while the blitzkrieg tore rapidly through the republics of the western USSR, the German ambassador Von Der Schulenberg handed his government's official declaration of war to the Soviet Foreign Commissar, that wily old diplomat Vyacheslav Mikhailovitch Molotov, Molotov looked at him in stunned amazement and asked merely: 'Why did you do it?'

Whatever the manifold reasons, there was one simple, awful result. Within five short weeks of the German invasion of Russia in 1941, the number of Jews murdered in Europe exceeded the total number of Jews killed in all of the previous eight tortuous years of Nazi rule. Within Lithuania 200,000 of the country's estimated 234,000 Jews were killed between July and November 1941. These figures represented a small fraction of the millions who would be exterminated by the end of the war, but in substantial areas of the Ostland they meant the complete destruction of its Jewish population. They were killed not by gas or by the production-line mass murder of the concentration camps – that, also, came later. They were killed by hand, by rifle, by machine-gun, and by .7 pistols.

And they were not all killed by Germans. From the main office of the Reich security forces in Berlin, from the SS, were created mobile battalions of Einsatzgruppen and Order Police, whose job was to follow on the heels of the frontline troops and enforce the policies of the Reich. These Order Police were quickly reinforced by those who the Germans dubbed 'Hiwis';

Hilfswillige, local volunteers often recruited from the prisoner-of-war camps of newly occupied territories and enlisted on the specific understanding that they would not be ordered to fight against Russians.

There were also, within weeks, within days of the launch of Operation Barbarossa, national labour defence battalions created, often out of partisan brigades and usually containing soldiers from the formerly independent armed forces of Estonia, Latvia, and Lithuania. They became known as auxiliary police battalions, and two of them were formed in Lithuania in July 1941. Juozas Janos Aleksynas joined one of these battalions immediately. 'There was a call-up of young people,' he would say later, 'and my understanding – I think most people's understanding – was that this was to provide internal order within Lithuania and generally help the war effort. The word was that you were only required to serve six months, and I thought that if I responded to this call-up then this was for me the best way to serve.'

Twelve months later Aleksynas deserted from his Lithuanian auxiliary battalion. 'It was clear,' he said, 'that I would be required to serve the Germans in a very incorrect and barbaric and inhuman way, which I was not prepared to do. It was clear that our job, the orders the Germans were giving us, was simply the mass extermination of people.'

In July 1941 the ruddy-faced, religious junior lieutenant from Jakuliai, Antanas Gecevicius, also joined the 2nd Lithuanian Auxiliary Battalion. His career would take him into White Russia, where he would be awarded the German Iron Cross. In 1944 he would flee with his battalion south to Italy, and there give himself up to the Allies. Once there, he would claim, he joined a Polish unit and fought against the Germans for the last few months of the war, gaining, bizarrely, a Polish Iron Cross to add to his German medal. Antanas Gecevicius's war would lead him to unpredictable situations.

Rising slowly to his feet and stuffing the spilt coins back into his pocket, Bob Tomlinson focused gradually on the tall man in the gloomy hallway. He extended a hand.

'Mr Gecas,' said Tomlinson, 'I'm here about the allegations. You have been named, as you know. You are in yesterday's *Sunday Times*. I would like to give you the opportunity to put your side of the story and tell me exactly what happened.'

He was taken through into a living-room and offered a seat. He was given coffee, more coffee on top of the endless cups he had already swallowed outside in the car, until the stuff was coursing through him like liquid fire and he longed to go to the toilet but dared not do so, dare not give Antony Gecas a minute alone to reflect, to telephone his lawyer, to think about saying No, go away.

For two hours Tomlinson talked what he hoped was pleasant gibberish. He talked about the weather, about houses, about the press, about anything, just so that silence did not hold dominion in Antony Gecas's living-room. And as 10.30 approached, Gecas agreed to the interview. But not until that afternoon, not until 2.30 p.m.

The crew came into the house at 10.30. Tomlinson gave cameraman Malcolm Campbell a surreptitious wink, and promptly began to hector him. 'Put that gear down, out of the way. Mr Gecas will see us, but not until this afternoon, and I don't want him upset. Put that equipment in this corner and leave it there. Mr Gecas, thank you for your help, and I'm sorry for any inconvenience. We'll return at half past two.' Then they left, in the comforting knowledge that Antony Gecas had either to throw a mobile camera unit's equipment out into the garden, or readmit its owners later in the day.

They did not take their eyes off the house. For four hours they sat in two cars at either end of Moston Terrace, sending people away for sandwiches and soup, and hoping that they were not seen. At 2.30 p.m. they returned to No. 3 and were readmitted. They assembled the unit and, sitting opposite each other in two armchairs, Antony Gecas and Bob Tomlinson commenced the interview which would change both of their lives.

From the very first question and the first firm and instant answer, Tomlinson was thrown. This was not an ordinary interviewee. This was not some ordinary criminal or accountant caught with his fingers in the till. Tomlinson knew that type, and he knew their standard response to allegations of guilt: the attempts at scorn, the rising and walking to the window and standing quietly in thought, the demands to know who made these accusations . . . Antony Gecas was a different calibre of suspect altogether. He hardly drew breath before an answer. He did not throw up his hands in horror and say My God! Me? He did not condemn the evil which had been done, nor did he insist that such evil was beyond his capability. It quickly became clear to Tomlinson, as they talked and as the camera rolled, that this man had been preparing for this interview for 45 years of his life.

'You signed a statement,' said Tomlinson, 'in front of Edinburgh police, to the effect that you witnessed the shooting of approximately 150 people. Did you take any part in that shooting?'

'Absolutely none.' Gecas's thick accent, dubbed with a Scottish burr, rolled confidently over the consonants. 'Because we were defending Germans who were doing it. And we did not know what they were shooting. There were in – ' he grasped for the words but continued to answer ' – these . . . villages . . . towns . . . forests . . . And the secret police, and the Gestapo, and local police, they were asking if these people were somewhere else or what. And then they were shooting, while we were doing duties outside, maybe mile or two mile outside the area.'

There was no confusion of names and no consideration of an answer. There was no request to repeat a place or to locate an occasion. This meeting has not come as a shock, thought Tomlinson. You knew somebody was going to knock on the

door. You didn't know who. It's me, but you didn't know who
it was going to be. You just knew, against all hope, that
somebody, sometime, would knock.

'Were you aware that in protecting the Germans you were
helping them shoot and murder innocent people?' asked
Tomlinson.

'Yes, I was aware, but what we could do about it? If we
didn't do, they would shoot us.'

'But you are aware that in protecting the Germans you
were in fact allowing them to carry on the murder of innocent
people?'

Antony Gecas leaned forward, his face a portrait of
confused, hurt innocence. 'How we know?' he protested.
'There was a war. The shooting start in a forest or in a village.
You don't know what's happening.'

Just following orders, thought Tomlinson, and now I am
more than 50 per cent sure that you have done something
terrible that you have always known that you are going to
have to answer to. Now, you are a serious target.

'What fear,' he asked, 'would you have about being tried
for these alleged crimes.'

Antony Gecas's answer was out of his mouth before
Tomlinson had stopped speaking. 'No fear whatsoever,' he
said.

Then he began sorrowfully shaking his head. 'I have no
fear whatsoever,' he repeated. 'But there will be no fair trial in
Russia, that's out of the question.' His voice rose emphatically
on the last four words. Conveniently, thought Tomlinson, the
Soviet Union is the only country in the world where, at
present, you could be tried.

'There will be nothing else,' Gecas continued on the
horrific prospect of a Soviet trial. 'You confess, you tell . . .
everything you tell. They beat you up, torture, and you tell
everything they want to tell. In this country, in other countries
you could have witnesses, and they tell, and they take evidence – not the Russians.'

What are you not telling me? thought Tomlinson as he made his thanks and farewells and the camera crew packed to leave. I have been wrong-footed. You have been waiting to answer these questions for a very long time and I have had a few weeks to prepare. You have done your homework; I am clutching at straws. You are answering as if to script, admitting to everything but guilt, your hands were everywhere but on the trigger. What, he thought again, are you not saying in that smooth defence?

But we have a story, the journalist consoled himself as the cars pulled away from Moston Terrace. Now, at least we have a story to pursue. Scottish Television broadcast the Gecas interview on its news bulletin that Monday evening, accompanied by the outraged reaction of a cantor from a Glasgow synagogue to the possibility that a war criminal was living peacefully, just 40 miles away.

And waiting there at Tomlinson's office were two further packages from Eli Rosenbaum. They contained details, sketchy but tantalising, of a bizarre conspiracy story. They hinted that since 1948 the British government had been operating an undercover system to help Nazi war criminals to evade justice. They suggested that successive governments, from the post-war Labour administration and the Conservative government led by Winston Churchill which followed it, up to the Thatcher regime of the 1980s, had actively sought to hide their former enemies in quiet neighbourhoods of Great Britain and the USA, and in the countries of the British Commonwealth.

His mind reeling, Tomlinson approached David Scott. 'We have to follow this through,' he insisted. 'David, we can't let it go. There's something here. God knows what, but there's something.'

Scott carefully considered the material. 'See what Rosenbaum will deliver,' he said finally. 'See if you can get Rosenbaum across with the goods.'

But before Eli Rosenbaum, attorney to the World Jewish

Congress in New York, and formerly of the United States
government's Office of Special Investigations, could arrive in
Scotland, the London embassy of the Union of Soviet Socialist
Republics had picked up the telephone.

4

'Mr Shabannikov,' said Bob Tomlinson to the first secretary at the Soviet Embassy in London, 'perhaps I had better make my position clear from the start. I am not a communist and I am not a Jew. I don't like communism. I don't like the USSR. I don't trust you and our viewers won't trust you either, and that's not my fault, it's your own. I am not saying I'm not Jewish because of any pride in the fact. I just am not. I'm not chasing this story because I'm Jewish, and I'm not doing it because I'm a communist. But I do want to get to the bottom of it all.'

The dark-haired, modest individual across the palatial wood-panelled room nodded gravely. 'I understand that,' he said.

Stranger and stranger, thought Tomlinson. He could be a nice guy.

It was not usual for the representatives of Moscow to telephone British journalists and offer their help with a news story; and it was highly unusual for any journalistic foot-soldier to be courted by so eminent a diplomat as Guennadi Shabannikov, the USSR's first secretary in London. But that November, a month after the exposure of and first interview with Antony Gecas, Bob Tomlinson was growing accustomed to the unusual.

The Soviet Embassy had telephoned Scottish Television shortly after their initial news programmes. They had further

information, they said, which might help the television station
with its inquiries. 'But it's difficult,' Shabannikov had protested, 'it's difficult on the telephone . . .'

So Bob Tomlinson and Simon Forrest made the journey
south and entered, under the fluttering red flag with its white
hammer and sickle, the elegant Georgian portals of the Kensington home of the USSR. They were taken into the foyer and
asked to wait. A man whose type would become familiar to
Tomlinson in the months to come sat at a desk by the foyer
door. He was dressed in a cheap, off-the-peg suit and his
cream, outdated shirt was worn at the collar and cuffs. He said
nothing, he hardly recognised their presence, and he wrote
endlessly as the visitors looked at each other and waited. He
was simply the man at the door, and everywhere that Tomlinson would go in the dying years of the Soviet Union in the last
third of the 1980s, the Scot would find one of his breed sitting
there, by an entrance, writing.

Tomlinson and Forrest picked up the pamphlets on the
coffee-table and flicked through them. They extolled the wonders of Soviet agriculture. They waited, well past the appointed
time. That also would become a familiar experience. Tomlinson
became convinced that it was a deliberate ploy, to ensure that
visitors read every available magazine on the wonders of Soviet
agriculture and the achievements of the country's basketball
teams.

They were eventually shown into a room the size of a
council house and seated on upholstered furniture, and with
the hidden microphones whirring tactfully in some quiet
corner (Tomlinson never did spot the electronics, after many a
meeting in these drawing-rooms, but it was always a matter of
some interest to him how, in their future conversations,
Guennadi Shabannikov could quote lengthily and verbatim
from that first meeting), they began to do business with the
first secretary.

'I understand that,' said Shabannikov. 'But one moment,
and I will give you a list of another 34 residents of Great

Britain who are wanted in our country to stand trial for war crimes.'

Tomlinson drew a breath. Where's this going? A month ago there weren't any war criminals in Britain; they all went to South America. We knew that because we'd seen it in the movies. Now the Simon Weisenthal Centre's fingered 17, and this guy at the Soviet Embassy's about to list another 34. That's 51 – we're tripping over them in the street. Where is it going to end?

'Out of this 34,' said Tomlinson, 'who do you want the most?'

'Kyrylo Zvaritch,' said Shabannikov.

'Tell us about Kyrylo Zvaritch.'

'He is known as the Beast of Borosov. He murdered children in the presence of their mothers. Zvaritch burnt down a house with people in it who were having a wedding celebration. He used to bury people alive. The people in Ukraine have been saying about him since that time, a wild beast, not a man. He perpetrated crimes against humanity.'

'Where is Kyrylo Zvaritch?'

'Bolton. He lives in Bolton.' Shabannikov continued evenly. 'The people of Ukraine have appealed to the British authorities that these criminals be brought to justice.'

'What was the response to that appeal?'

'The response was negative.'

'If we want to take this any further,' said Tomlinson, 'can we go to your country?'

'Of course. You have shown an honest interest. We will allow your crew, but no others.'

'I will call you back and tell you when,' said Tomlinson, thinking, all we have to do now is clear this with David Scott. Tomlinson and Forrest left the embassy and went to a nearby public house where, with two hours before their flight back to Scotland, they wondered aloud how far out of control this story was likely to be blown. So many powers: the United States, the USSR, Israel, all trying to get hold of this mush-

rooming number of war criminals apparently steadfastly protected, through thick and thin, by Whitehall and Downing
Street. Never mind where it was likely to stop – where did it
start, where did they begin to grasp this mad, incomprehen-
sible chain of events?

In Scotland the decision was then taken to make a half-
hour documentary on the subject of the lost and lonely men
who were scattered, apparently, across Great Britain, whose
hands if not consciences were stained with the most terrible
crimes of the Second World War. Ross Wilson would direct,
and for the moment there would be no need to leave Great
Britain. Because in talking, and looking at each other in
occasional bemused, wondering silences, at least one of the
answers had seemed to dawn. Rosenbaum had said that it all
went back to 1948, to that cover-up – to the gigantic iceberg
which lay submerged beneath this small, visible crest.

Eli Rosenbaum flew into Glasgow on a ferocious winter's night
in December 1986. Snow and ice had brought the city to a
standstill, approach roads were blocked and main roads were
effectively impassable. His flight from New York was the last
aeroplane allowed to land at Glasgow airport that day. Tomlinson and Forrest met him there, a tall, unruffled figure, deep
voiced and carefully spoken, the essence – as Ephraim Zuroff
had suggested – of a young Manhattan lawyer. He was
carrying, as hand-luggage, a locked attaché-case.

With Glasgow at a standstill the three men booked into an
airport hotel. And there, on the bed in his room, Eli Rosenbaum
laid out the Ratline documents. Ratline, he explained, had
become colloquial, ironic shorthand for the system put in place
by the governments of Britain and the United States at the end
of the war proper, and the beginning of the Cold War, covertly
to remove and hide suspected war criminals from their pur-
suers in the Soviet bloc. It was a perverse underground railway,
a strange mockery of the way that victims of the Nazis had
themselves been smuggled secretly away from the clutches of

their persecutors. But the function of Ratline was not to protect the innocent. It was to conceal those who were probably guilty, just another curious black twist in the labyrinthine manoeuvres of that long post-war stand-off between East and West. There before them, scattered across the neatly pressed bedspread, were the residual pieces of a jigsaw which had lain unattended since 1948. They were unpromising, routine documents: letters in the large, bold serif of an old typewriter, and apparently mundane telegrams and memos. But their significance leaped out of every written word.

They were classified Top Secret in Great Britain. There was a telegram from Philip Noel-Baker, Secretary of State for Commonwealth Relations in 1948, concerning 'traitors and collaborators' in Commonwealth-occupied post-war Europe:

> In general, no fresh trials should be started after 31 August 1948. This would particularly affect cases of alleged war criminals not now in custody who might subsequently come into our hands. In our view, the punishment of war criminals is more a matter of discouraging future generations than of meting out retribution to every guilty individual. It is now necessary to dispose of the past as soon as possible.

Noel-Baker had followed this telegram with a letter, dated 13 July 1948, to the governments of Canada, Australia, New Zealand, South Africa, India, Pakistan and Ceylon:

> We are anxious that all extraditions arising out of the war should be brought to an end as soon as possible. All applications by foreign powers for extradition of persons alleged to have committed acts of treason or collaborated with the enemy during the period of occupation by the armed forces of Germany or her allies, should be presented on or before 1 January 1949.

He had effectively told the Commonwealth to stop Nazi-hunting. He had, equally effectively, made half of the globe a safe haven for war criminals.

Here, indeed, was a story. Here was a clutch of stories. 'In 1961,' said Rosenbaum, to the journalists personally and then later on camera, 'a request was made of the British government for the extradition of a man named Mere, an Estonian national who was wanted for the mass murder of some 125,000 human beings at the Ogala concentration camp and related sub-camps in Nazi-occupied Estonia. British authorities said, "No", there is no extradition treaty in this case; and moreover "an unduly long period of time has elapsed since the commission of the offence".

'Later that year, Mere was tried in absentia in the Soviet Union, was convicted, and was sentenced to death. He died living in peace in the United Kingdom a few years later. He was never, ever brought to justice.'

And then, there was the case of Dr Vladislav Dering, OBE . . . 'A man,' said Rosenbaum, 'who was involved in the most notorious of – quote – sterilisation experiments – unquote – on men and women prisoners at the Auschwitz death camp during the war; a man who constantly performed surgery on these victims.

'We now have a newly discovered document.' He held it up. 'The recently declassified Central Registry of War Criminals, on which Dr Dering's name appears, listed as "Wanted For Torture". And under the column "Wanted by . . ." there is a one-word entry: "UK". In 1948, which is to say later in the same year that the Central Registry was issued, his extradition was formally requested by Poland, on whose territory of course Auschwitz was located, and the British authorities said, "No".

'They then employed the man as a doctor in the colonial service in Somalia, awarded him, of all things, the OBE, and then allowed him to move to London, where he set up a very lucrative medical practice treating private patients. He died much later in London, despite having been exposed in 1963. The British government well knew who he was, and took absolutely no action to disturb the quietude of his life.

'So time and again,' concluded Rosenbaum, his tone

measured and his earnest brow furrowed, 'when the presence in the UK of accused Nazi war criminals has been brought to the attention of the British authorities, they have declined to take any action whatsoever, and for many, many years have been saying, "an unduly long period of time has elapsed since the commission of the crime". That very language was used in October by Minister of State Tim Renton about another individual living in Bolton . . .'

It was Zvaritch! Guennadi Shabannikov's Beast of Borosov! What does go on down those corridors of power? '. . . whom the UK authorities refused to extradite,' continued Rosenbaum, 'back in 1971, when his surrender to stand trial on war-crimes charges was first demanded. So nothing, I'm saddened to say, has changed.'

The action of the Simon Weisenthal Centre in releasing that information about 17 war criminals hidden in Britain had urged bodies other than the media into life. Following the events of October, an All-Party Parliamentary War Crimes Group had been established by a collection of interested Members of Parliament. It was chaired by the Labour MP and former Home Secretary, the affable Merlyn Rees. Armed with his Ratline documents, Tomlinson went to call on Rees.

Rees ran his fingers through his hair and shook his head slightly. 'I would be horrified if that was the case,' he said. 'But I am sure that that's the sort of information, if it came to light, that the committee would be very anxious to see. I'm surprised that happened, because while there were large numbers of people on the periphery, there must have been serious war criminals who still could have been pursued.'

Another member of the All-Party War Crimes Group, Greville Janner – an MP half of whose family had been incinerated in the holocaust and who was, as a consequence, less inclined than most to suggest that these things are best forgotten – was less astonished. 'I think,' he offered, 'that the governments of the day felt that they'd had enough and were looking round for other enemies. I suspect that once the war with the Germans was won there were some people who said, "Oh, well, who's the real enemy now: it's the Russians", and so anybody who dislikes the Russians is all right with us.'

Bob Tomlinson first met Professor Gerald Draper in the Green Park Hotel, Park Lane, London. The name of this elderly authority on jurisprudence, who had served with the Nuremburg prosecution and had sustained a life-long interest in the cases of war criminals, had become unavoidable, and Tomlinson and Ross Wilson had come to expect a great deal from him. An academic, authoritative, non-political line from a logician of the British school, a careful, avuncular assessment of their story and of their case . . . they awaited Professor Draper, that winter's day in London's West End, with anticipation. It was not just his eminence, his position as legal adviser to the War Crimes Group, his role as Professor of Law at Essex University. It was that here, surely, would be a man who could – on camera – put this byzantine issue into context, who could help to decipher the hieroglyphics.

Philip Rubenstein, the secretary of the All-Party War Crimes Group, arranged the meeting. On the night before, Tomlinson and Wilson had an agitated discussion about the story they were uncovering. It was apparently bigger, so much bigger, than a single half-hour slot on Britain being a safehouse for Nazi war criminals. It was becoming difficult to discuss the present project without dwelling on its seeming inadequacy, and Wilson left the London hotel with a ticket to see *Phantom of the Opera* while Tomlinson sat alone in the hotel restaurant, unable to eat. Pre-match nerves, he told himself. Pre-match nerves, before even a 'friendly' interviewee . . .

On the following morning the crew set up their equipment in a hotel room while Wilson and Tomlinson sat downstairs, preparing to meet Gerald Draper. Suddenly it occurred to them that they had no idea how to recognise their man in a lobby busy with well-dressed, patrician gentlemen. No identifying folded copies of the *Financial Times* had been pre-arranged, no red carnations. None of the people who had spoken to them of the depth of this man's knowledge – including a Scottish Television staffer to whom he had taught law – had mentioned his appearance.

At about 11 a.m. a very old man, stooped at the waist, bent almost into an L-shape with his torso virtually parallel with the ground, accompanied by a distinguished-looking lady entered the foyer of the Green Park Hotel. One of the crew looked at Tomlinson and Wilson and quipped. 'Just our luck if that's him.'

It was. As they walked slowly upstairs, with the Scottish Television personnel ashamedly wondering how on earth they were going to get this gentleman on to camera, it became apparent that Professor Draper's stoop was not the arthritic disfigurement of age. Tomlinson would only learn its true cause later.

And when Draper sat down on a chair in the filming room his body arched backwards and instantly upright and his posture became erect and commanding. He sat like a guardsman in the chair, his bright eyes flickered, and the grace of his personality and the clarity of his intellect absorbed the camera and captured irredeemably the attention of everybody in the room. He spoke with precision and a clipped economy of words, and his comments were invested with both dignity and a passion that was all the more moving by being constrained into the language of reason and of the law.

In 1943, said Draper, the three Allied leaders, Churchill, Stalin and Roosevelt, aware by then of the terrible deeds which were being enacted under the flag of the Third Reich, had signed a treaty in Moscow agreeing that upon the cessation of hostilities war criminals should be hunted down.

'It was a declaration, subscribed to by the Three, in order to establish the principle of the policy of what was going to be the United Nations: that the war criminals of the Nazi Axis would be brought to face their crimes, back in the countries where these abominations had been committed, and they would be made to answer for them.

'The United Kingdom,' continued Professor Draper in tones that brooked no argument, 'through its Foreign Office, had a list of the hundred worst Nazis. And if any of these evil men fell into the hands of the United Kingdom government, they would be shot. Humanely and swiftly. But the indictment would be read to them first.

'In the early days the revulsion of the British public from what they had seen of the film of the Belsen trials, which was shown fairly early on, I think in Leicester Square, was obviously something that no government could ignore, and people were demanding as swift as possible a trial of the people who had run that particular hell-hole.'

'Later on, as the climate of opinion shifted and the winds changed in Europe, approaching the Berlin airlift and the revival of Western Germany, and all the difficulties of the Cold War, a different approach was found in government policy, and there was a cooling of the attitude of government towards war criminals . . .'

Between 1943 and 1948 there was a policy change around 180 degrees of the compass. Tomlinson asked Draper if he knew of any of the individual cases which had been mentioned so far in the course of Scottish Television's researches. At the mention of Dr Vladislav Dering, OBE, the old man smiled grimly.

'He was a doctor, and he had been captured and ended up in a concentration camp. He was released for doing an extremely unpleasant series of a revolting operation called ovarectomy on young Jewish Salonika girls in the age group 16, 17, 18 – the removal of their ovaries under a local novocaine injection in the spine.

'And Dr Dering, having done so well in this field, was released from the camp. And that was big news – in his tailor-made suit and laced-up shoes and two heavy suitcases. That was not the normal way a prisoner left Auschwitz.' Professor Draper's eyes gleamed with a sudden deep anger. 'He normally left it' – his voice dropped and he articulated the words slowly – 'up the chimney.

'He came to Britain after the war, and he ended up in Scotland, where he took part in a Christmas mess party with some Polish officers. That must have been the first Christmas after the end of the war. And Dering was a little addicted to the brandy, and he got rather tight. And under the influence of drink Dering pointed to the suit he was wearing and said, "Do you see this suit? It's an excellent suit, some of the best material in Europe. It belonged to a Dutch professor. He went up the chimney. Do you see my pipe wallet? Do you see that? I got that from a prisoner. It's made out of a prisoner's scrotum."'

As the crew folded away their equipment and Professor Gerald Draper stood once again, a small, bent figure, Tomlinson said, 'What was it, professor? Did you have an accident, or a stroke?'

Draper placed his right hand gently on the journalist's forearm, like a doctor about to break bad news to a patient. 'Mr Tomlinson,' he said, 'when I started investigating and prosecuting war criminals in Germany I walked as tall and as straight as you. After it all, I was like this. To this day the doctors don't know why . . .' He hesitated, and then continued, 'So if you are going to go down this road, be very careful. It could have a very serious effect upon you.'

It was a remark, kindly offered, which Tomlinson never forgot. In the blackest moments of what was to come those chilling words returned: the advice of an ally rather than the warning of a foe, to keep a distance from the insuperable burden of atrocity.

Draper had, in the end, exceeded their high expectations. Wilson and Tomlinson left his company finally convinced of their government's complicity in hiding war criminals and protecting them from justice. Draper was not optimistic that the law could be changed to alter this situation, despite permitting himself the spoken thought that 'with my knowledge and your enthusiasm, perhaps something can be achieved.' He would not live to see it, but his last hope was realised.

In the meantime, the trail of the Beast of Borosov, Kyrylo Zvaritch, went quite literally dead. Tomlinson's investigations among the crumbling cotton mills of Bolton in the north of England revealed that all of the Soviet Union's requests for extradition, all of the All-Party War Crimes Group's letters to the government, all of the Simon Weisenthal Centre's interest was finally – in Zvaritch's case – pointless. Zvaritch had died in a Bolton hospital in 1984. Like Vladislav Dering, he had never been officially investigated by the British government. Like Dering, and God only knew how many others, he had never been asked to face the scales of justice and answer his accusers. Once again, the secret plans of 1947 had, 40 years on, proved successful.

Where did that leave the pensioner living quietly as a perfect neighbour in the Edinburgh suburbs, the man whose name had first prompted Tomlinson to board this rollercoaster: Antanas Gecas, aka Gecevicius?

'Mr Gecas,' the Weisenthal Centre's spokesman had told a press conference in Israel, 'is accused of mass murder. He lives in Edinburgh. He is a mining engineer. And we have the documentation . . .'

'The Gecas case,' said Greville Janner, 'as I said in the House of Commons – he is alleged to be a very serious war criminal. He has made himself certain admissions, and he is certainly very high on the list of priorities of those who feel that something should be done.'

There was a grey area here still. How serious a war criminal did Antanas Gecas have to be, before he indubitably merited the attentions of the legal system – or, indeed, the time of Scottish Television?

'By virtue of his helping the Germans to carry [war crimes] out,' argued Eli Rosenbaum, 'in terms of protecting the Germans from rear-area attack, and of preventing the victims from escaping by encircling the area of the execution, he participated directly in the crimes even though he may not have pulled the trigger.'

'What we could do about it?' Gecas had protested. 'If we didn't do, they would shoot us.'

'On the basis of what he has admitted,' pursued Rosenbaum, 'let me suggest an analogy. If you and I go to someone's house here in Glasgow to kill him, and we agree that you will do the actual killing and that my task is to lock all the doors in the house and stand guard, so that if anyone comes you will not be interfered with as you carry out this killing, you and I will be held by any court in Scotland to be equally complicit in this act of murder. Because I have enabled you to carry out the crime, and have prevented the victim from escaping. That is a standard tenet of Anglo-Saxon common law.

'There is no doubt at all in my mind, and I don't think there was any doubt in the minds of my colleagues at the United States Department of Justice. Frankly, what shocked us was not just the fact that he was living here and that our interview with him in 1982 was after all conducted in the presence of the Lothian and Borders Police, but that it did not lead to any kind of investigation or to any kind of action on the part of the UK authorities.'

Gerald Draper concurred that the thick official blanket which had been thrown across the shoulders of Antanas Gecas should be jerked away. 'Assuming that the evidence is that he was an active, consistent participant,' mused the professor, 'in the deliberate extermination of Jews in the former Baltic states by mass shooting, sometimes called "sonderaction", and that those allegations exist, and that there is evidence to support them, I see no reason whatsoever why this gentleman should have his crimes looked over.'

'I would want to put him on trial,' said former Home Secretary Merlyn Rees. 'I would get the best lawyers available to say, Where can he be put on trial? Can he be extradited? If he has become a British citizen, can his citizenship be taken away from him? I would want to not move on my emotions, but I would want my emotions to drive me to get the best information so that I could do something about it.'

These nice distinctions of Anglo-Saxon common law, these well-intentioned gropings towards establishing the level of offence of any participant in the holocaust, these efforts to determine even the possibility of prosecution would, sooner than any of the speakers could have guessed, become redundant – swept away by a weight of new evidence and by an astonishing change of government policy. But in the winter of 1986–87, to people still stumbling on the lower slopes of mountainous events, they were important. They gave a foothold. More than that, they helped to establish base camp.

Tomlinson and his colleagues spent a good part of that winter attempting to elicit a response from the Home Office in London to their fattening file of evidence, hearsay, opinion and damning historical documentation. Both the Home and Foreign offices refused to give an interview, on or off camera.

But after no fewer than 78 telephone calls from Glasgow, the Home Office issued a statement. It said: 'We have never received a request in respect of an alleged war criminal from a country with which we have an extradition treaty. We have no such treaty with the Soviet Union or Israel.'

'I don't think that people would put that argument,' commented Greville Janner, 'if like myself, half their family had been murdered. In my case, brought together in a synagogue, and they set alight to the synagogue and burnt them all. There isn't any statute of limitations on murder anyway. The memory ought to be kept alive because this kind of inhumanity can recur. I was a war-crimes investigator in Germany in the British Army at the time when the unit was disbanded in 1949. And we knew that there were thousands of war criminals on the loose. And I've always thought that it was a very wicked world that would allow people like that to sleep in their beds at night, in peace, after the murders they'd committed.'

'If the government in London does not hear from the people,' concluded Eli Rosenbaum reluctantly, 'that this injustice must be righted, then I suspect that nothing will be done. The British policy of non-interest in Nazi war crimes will be continued.'

Before he flew back to New York, Eli Rosenbaum was taken by Bob Tomlinson to Moston Terrace in Edinburgh to meet Antanas Gecas. Tomlinson telephoned the house beforehand, to ask if he could call in on a certain afternoon. He did not mention his guest. As they walked along the snow-covered semi-detached street, the elegant Rosenbaum was faintly nervous. 'I've come 3,000 miles,' he said, almost to himself as the front door drew closer, 'let's see him . . .'

Tomlinson knocked on the door and it was quickly opened by Mrs Gecas. 'Hello,' said the journalist cheerfully. 'Is Mr Gecas in? Bob Tomlinson – I said I'd drop in and see him.' The two men crossed the threshold. A dog barked.

'This is Eli,' said Tomlinson to Gecas. 'Eli is from America. He's investigating all the cases.'

Antanas Gecas backed off and began to push the door against them. 'Sorry,' he said, 'I'm not listening.'

'I work for the US Department of Justice,' said Eli Rosenbaum as he reversed out into the street.

'Nothing. Nothing to say,' added Antanas Gecas.

'There'll come a time when questions will have to be asked,' said Eli Rosenbaum, 'and the answers will have to be given.'

The door slammed shut.

Britain, The Nazi Safehouse was broadcast across Great Britain on Channel 4 and in Scottish Television's *Scottish Report* slot on 29 January 1987. A taut documentary, crackling with material and alive with the tension of answered questions, it achieved an instant response from the public and the rest of the media.

Newspapers across Britain headlined its revelations across their news, rather than their review, pages. Readers of the

Bolton Evening News were informed that the man some of them had known as 'Stanislaw Piotrowski, a retired landlord of Bromwich Street, Bolton, who died in Hulton Lane Hospital in January 1984, aged 73' was in fact wanted in the Ukraine as Kyrylo Zvaritch, the Beast of Borosov. The *Wolverhampton Press and Star* quoted Greville Janner as saying that he was prepared to 'name names' of other wanted men in the House of Commons. Several national tabloids simply summarised the programme's contents and ran them, paragraph after paragraph, as page-head stories.

Others, in a taste of what was to come within 12 short months, picked up the issue and ran with it. The high-circulation *Daily Mirror* chose to editorialise on the subject. 'Eight months ago in Jerusalem,' pronounced its leader column . . .

> Mrs Thatcher brushed away a tear after visiting a museum dedicated to the six million holocaust victims. Today, she goes on brushing aside requests for help in prosecuting Nazi war criminals hiding here. She is following the policy of every government since 1948 – when Ratline was set up to save important Nazis from the fate they deserved.
>
> Despite their torture and mass murder of the innocent, they were spread through Britain, the Commonwealth and America to help the West to rearm to face a new enemy, Russia . . . On Channel 4 on Wednesday night, a Scottish TV production – *Britain, The Nazi Safehouse* – identified some of the 17 men Jewish hunters say were war criminals – and against whom the government refuses to act . . . [the Ratline's] poison is a betrayal of the millions who died in the concentration camps and on the battlefields.
>
> Time can't wipe away the crimes – these men must be brought to justice.

To Tomlinson, still new to television and shy of personal publicity, the experience was nerve-wracking. On the day of broadcast, press conferences had been called in both London and Glasgow, the former held by Scottish Television's head of PR in the capital, and the latter by David Scott and a brilliant young press officer named Eileen Gallacher, who became Director of Broadcasting at Scottish Television, and whose capacity for absorbing the essence of a story and then disseminating it was remarked upon by all.

Tomlinson avoided both venues, and turned down radio interviews. Fully alive to the importance of their researches and to the impact that their film was likely to make, Ross Wilson and Bob Tomlinson shuddered at the preying doubts that small errors might exist in their work, that this enormous edifice might be collapsed by tiny faults. Their fears were not helped by the fact that during filming they had tracked down one Professor Poppe, the first man ever to be shipped out along the Ratline. An American photojournalist had taken pictures of Poppe, and they were included in the film. They told Rosenbaum of this on the telephone, and he instantly and surprisingly said, 'You must take him out.'

'We can't. He's in, and it goes out in a few hours.'

'You must,' said Rosenbaum. 'Poppe is innocent. Poppe was taken out along the Ratline because the Soviets had claimed he was a war criminal. The British and US governments didn't think he was, and they took him to America, where he was "lost". And this time they were right. He was innocent. Erase him.'

Professor Poppe was duly erased, and the tension inside Scottish Television mounted as transmission time approached. Some leaks to the press had resulted in stories appearing which previewed the programme's exclusive material, but in London a leak of a more sinister variety occurred.

Part of Scottish Television's documentation had found its way into the hands of a reporter from a national quality daily. He in turn argued that the Ratline papers referred only to the western sector of Berlin and occupied Germany, not to Great Britain – Ratline, in other words, may have been just a mechanism for shifting men around within Germany. 'Check it out,' growled Scott.

And so it came about that as the press gathered in Glasgow to shout urgent questions to David Scott about *Britain, The Nazi Safehouse*, Bob Tomlinson was in an adjacent room, on the telephone trying to get through yet again to the reassuring oracle, Eli Rosenbaum, fighting to make himself heard above the neighbouring din, sinking eventually to his knees and crawling, with the telephone clutched tightly against his ear, under the sound-proofing of an office desk.

'Eli? . . . Eli? Have we got the Ratline wrong? The *Daily Telegraph* are saying we have got it wrong, that Ratline only applied within Germany. Just tell me, have we got it wrong?'

Rosenbaum's calm, assured, Manhattan attorney's voice came over the line like a balm. 'You haven't got it wrong. For God's sake, tell me: when was the last trial of a war criminal in Great Britain? When was a war criminal last investigated in Great Britain? When was a war criminal last extradited from Great Britain? If anyone thinks that Ratline applied only to Berlin and to occupied Germany, just ask them those questions. You have got it right.'

Tomlinson crawled out from underneath the table. He jotted down the words 'We've got it right' on a slip of paper, gave it to one of David Scott's secretarial staff to deliver into the mayhem of the adjoining press conference, and then he fled to the safety of his own office.

5

The fateful decision to make a second, longer documentary on the subject was taken within weeks. Tomlinson and Wilson were more agitated by the insufficiency of *Britain, The Nazi Safehouse* than they were thrilled by its success. Their sense of being on the edge of a bigger, more important story, that teetering feeling which had so disturbed them in the Green Park Hotel on the night before their meeting with Professor Gerald Draper, had not diminished. The press, public and governmental response to *Britain, The Nazi Safehouse* fuelled the flames. Above all, it was clear that the old man in Moston Terrace, Antanas Gecas, had more to tell than he had permitted himself, thus far, to reveal.

Early in 1987 events were also achieving a dynamic outside the television studios. Two rabbis connected with the Simon Weisenthal Centre had flown from Los Angeles to meet with Douglas Hurd, the Home Secretary, armed with a list of questions about Britain's strange, dilatory stance on the subject of Nazi war criminals.

One of them, Rabbi Marvin Hier, held a press conference in Westminster, just over the road from the House of Commons. Media interest ran high, and the conference was oversubscribed with eager journalists. Scottish Television's offices were deluged with calls from local papers and radio stations, all anxious to know if one of the 17 Weisenthal names lived in their neck of the woods. (A decision was taken in Glasgow to co-operate with bona fide publications and broadcasters and give them the required information: not to have done so, it was reasoned, would have put Scottish Television in bed with all the other official liars, concealers, and obfuscators.) Inquiries came in from Australia, Canada, New Zealand . . .

'You've got the answers,' said David Scott to Tomlinson. 'You'd better speak to them.' So the journalist found himself being interviewed through satellite links on live talk-shows in the Antipodes, North America, and the Caribbean.

Tomlinson also travelled south to Marvin Hier's Westminster press conference, and met the rabbi beforehand. 'How far do you intend to go?' asked Hier.

'As far as we can. But we need all the assistance we can get. It's not a crusade on our part – we're just journalists; programme-makers.'

Shortly before Hier's crowded conference was brought to order and begun, an Eastern European voice shouted over the mêlée: 'Is Bob Tomlinson here?'

'That's me.'

'Can I see you afterwards?'

'Sure.'

It was the bureau chief of the official Polish press agency. He offered to arrange a meeting in London with one Professor Kokol, the chairman of the Polish War Crimes Commission. 'Go to Poland,' added the Polish pressman. 'We'll open the archive there to you. You can help us track down men who have committed crimes in Poland.'

Was it never-ending?

On the following day the Home Secretary, Douglas Hurd, himself called a press conference, with the express intention of defusing the issue by denouncing the unofficial investigators. We have no evidence, said Hurd. We can do nothing on the basis of unsubstantiated allegations. We have no extradition treaty with the Soviet Union.

Sitting a few feet from the Home Secretary, Tomlinson thought: It's just a continuation of policy, the policy of every government since the end of the war. This came to the journalist as a surprisingly shocking and depressing revelation. We are, he thought glumly, just whistling in the wind. Hurd is saying, clear as day, that nothing is going to happen. We can wave as many documents at him as we like; wheel a small football crowd of witnesses on to camera; broadcast documentaries until we and our viewers are half-dead with boredom; and the government – well, the government is just going to sit tight. Why not? Sitting tight has served them well since 1948.

The questions of the southern press seemed gauged to help Hurd in his mission: sycophantic, ingratiating, yes sir, no sir, everybody seemed quite happy to be able to wander away and denounce the Weisenthal list, nobody was interested in looking at the substance . . .

'What about Scottish Television's programme, *Britain, The Nazi Safehouse*?' came a question from the floor.

Tomlinson looked up. Hurd brushed the question aside: '. . . allegations . . . no evidence . . .'

Simmering with anger, Tomlinson stuffed his notebook in his pocket, put his pen away, and got to his feet.

'My name is Bob Tomlinson,' he said to Hurd. 'I am from Scottish Television. Tell me, Home Secretary, when did we last investigate an alleged war criminal living in Great Britain?'

Douglas Hurd turned to one of his aides.

'It's a rhetorical question,' said Tomlinson. 'When did we last put an alleged war criminal on trial in Great Britain? Don't bother – that's another rhetorical question. When did we last convict a war criminal living in Britain? When are you going to do something about this?'

Hurd and Tomlinson looked at each other for several minutes, the one with unconcealed irritation at such defiance of the protocol of ministerial briefings, and the latter still furious. Douglas Hurd would eventually become the first British politician to grasp the nettle of war crimes, but that would be months and years ahead, and it seemed the most unlikely of eventualities in the dull hostility of the closing minutes of his first London press conference on the subject. Tomlinson's anger with this smooth, prevaricating politician in the late winter of 1987 was total and consuming.

When it became possible to see clearly, nothing could have been more obvious than the fact that *Britain, The Nazi Safehouse* had touched nerves: the nerves of sympathisers with its theme, the hardened nerves of the media, the sensibilities of the surprised public, and a raw and jangling nerve at the heart of government.

At that time Bob Tomlinson's office was a Portakabin in the carpark of Scottish Television. Sitting in that vulnerable little structure, while Glasgow buses passed by and passengers on the top deck looked idly down at the man on the telephone, he fielded calls from thousands of miles away on the subject of horrors that had occurred four decades ago, and frequently he felt like waving those passengers down from their seats and saying, here, come and listen to this. To take them into the empty Portakabin and thereby touch base with reality. Later he would realise that these susceptible human yearnings were prompted as much as anything else by the knowledge that this unstoppable story was going to lead to disaster for somebody. Who? Scottish Television? The government? Antanas Gecas? Bob Tomlinson? Having been started, it could not be stopped, and there would be – there could be – no joy at its end.

But the story drove its journalists now. They were securely in harness, and one thing above all had become clear: they were being urged out of the British Isles. Wherever else it led, this was no longer a British story alone. And the place to which they were pointed more than any other was that ramshackle, creaking, communist empire which Adolf Hitler had invaded in the June of 1941: the Union of Soviet Socialist Republics. The Portakabin in a Glasgow carpark was, Ross Wilson and Bob Tomlinson realised, becoming redundant. It was time to visit Moscow. It was time for Guennadi Shabanni-kov, first secretary at the Soviet Embassy in London, to deliver.

So Tomlinson found himself again walking under the

hammer and sickle and through the portals of that Kensington pile, again in a dusty foyer reading of the accomplishments of Soviet beet growers while an apparatchik scribbled endlessly by the door, again sitting in the cool, appraising gaze of the first secretary, again wondering where they hid the microphones . . .

'You asked some time ago,' said Shabannikov, 'if you could go to the Soviet Union. Do you have to go?'

Tomlinson breathed deep. 'If we are to pursue the story,' he said, 'I have to.'

'Are you going to pursue the story.'

'Yes.' The proper authority for this answer could be achieved later. 'Yes, we are going to pursue it.'

'I will make the arrangements. Telephone me when you are ready.'

'Every time I try to phone you,' said Tomlinson, 'I am told to call back later. If I phone at one, I am told to try at two. At two, I'm told three. At three, four . . .'

Shabannikov nodded, and handed a private number across the desk.

Tomlinson walked to the end of the street and telephoned David Scott from a public box. 'The Russians say we can go to the Soviet Union,' he said.

'Will they give you full access to everything?'

'I don't know. I just think that this guy is on our side.'

'Okay. Get the next flight back and we'll decide what we want from him.'

Tomlinson sat on the aeroplane scribbling notes, preparing his case for Scott and for the filming of a second programme. Beside him a burly trades unionist returning from a conference drank beer and attempted conversation.

'I've seen you before. On a demonstration?'

'Maybe. I'm a journalist. I might have been covering it.'

'Well, comrade . . .'

They didn't call me that in the Soviet Embassy, thought Tomlinson.

Scott and Tomlinson made up a shopping-list for Shaban-nikov. They wanted at least three witnesses to separate crimes. They wanted documentation. They wanted full access to any survivors. They wanted access to former colleagues of the accused, at liberty or in jail. And it must be soon.

'We are prepared to go and look for the material, with your co-operation,' said Tomlinson to Shabannikov. 'And this is what we want.'

'Yes,' said the first secretary. 'And you must contact the governor of Gostel Radio in Moscow. He will facilitate your trip. Telephone him; we will also speak to him from here; and when you are ready you may go.'

The decision to make the documentary which would change the law of Great Britain, which would take a Scottish court for the first time to sit behind the Iron Curtain, which would lead to a war-crimes trial in the coat of a civil action for the first time in Great Britain, and which did – as they had always known that it would – lead to personal humiliation and tragedy for at least one of its protagonists, was taken then in the offices of Scottish Television. An hour-long documentary to be titled *Crimes of War* was put underway. The footwork started again.

It began with cold and boredom and lack of sleep in the Portakabin in Scottish Television's carpark. For weeks Tomlinson dragged himself out of bed at four in the morning to report for work at an hour convenient to the Moscow time-zone; and for weeks he could get no response from the Russian radio station. Driven by the conviction that, if witnesses could be produced from Slutsk, Lithuania and whatever other killing grounds might litter those bleak and marshy plains, if people still there would stand and talk, then a story of kinds could be stitched together to shake the icy complacency of Douglas Hurd and rattle the windows of Whitehall, Tomlinson kept dialling until he was on first-name terms with the international operators, each of them possibly seated like him, before one-bar electric fires in the bitter, black hours before dawn, trying to make connections across the steppes of Eastern Europe.

'Moscow 9318332,' he would request, shivering in the Portakabin at 4.00 a.m. 'Moscow 9318332,' morning after stricken morning. 'That'll be 041–332 – ', 'Yes, Scottish Television, double-9 double-9 . . .', 'Problems in Prague this morning, Mr Tomlinson, but we'll keep trying.' This is the dash and romance of journalism, he thought, cowering over the single-bar fire and hearing the empty telephone line at his ear click, and click again, and stay empty. If you've the stamina to sit in a cold room without any coffee for four hours at a time, one day after the other, you can do this job.

Occasionally he did get through. When this happened nobody was in. 'But I've been told by the Soviet Embassy to phone this man at this number. Where is he?'

The anonymous voice at the other end of the line shrugged audibly. 'Five thousand people work in this building,' it said.

At the start of the third week, like a stranded hitch-hiker, Bob Tomlinson got lucky. His call rang out in Moscow, and a man picked it up who was to change the course of events.

'My name is Pavel Tsarvoulonov,' he said. 'Can I help you?'

'I would like to send you telexes,' said Tomlinson, 'concerning a possible trip to the Soviet Union by a Scottish Television crew, arranged with Guennadi Shabannikov at – '

'Yes, I know all about it.'

Tsarvoulonov was a journalist and translator who already had an interest in the war-crimes issue. 'Were you expecting my call?' asked Tomlinson.

'No. I was just passing the office when the phone rang.'

Communications improved marginally after that. There would still be no response, by telex or by telephone, from the Soviets to precise inquiries, no assurances that matters were being resolved and problems overcome. But there was, at least, always Tsarvoulonov.

'We can't just arrive on speculation,' said Tomlinson to the Russian one day. 'We have to know what is there.'

'I assure you, we are doing everything we can. This will all be in place. We will give it to you when you come.'

'Have they got what we want?' asked David Scott.

'David, they're telling me that we have to go there and get it.'

'We can't go over there in hope.'

'But they're saying, we will not get anything unless we go. I've told them we need hard facts, not just co-operation. But they keep saying, when you come here, we'll give it all to you.'

Scott nodded. 'Go and get it,' he said. 'And while you're there, carry out a full recce. Speak to everyone you have to speak to. Take as long as you need, just make sure you get it right. And if it doesn't stand up, forget it. You can let me know how it's going – when you call in, make good days champagne and bad ones just beer. If it's not going right, say you're off to the bar for a beer. You'll need it.'

Ross Wilson and Bob Tomlinson flew to Moscow in March 1987, vaguely hoping that somebody – anybody – at the state radio station would remember their names.

It was like arriving in the permanent twilight of Gotham City. They disembarked, after a deliberately sober flight, in the darkest part of the airport. Three-quarters of the terminal's electric lights had fused, and endless queues of people in identically anonymous dark overcoats shuffled along the freezing floor.

Tomlinson approached the soldier in the passport office and stood against a wall as his height was confirmed, and the soldier gazed interminably upon him. Tomlinson broke the deadlock by putting a pack of 20 Benson and Hedges cigarettes on the counter. The soldier smiled, took the cigarettes, and returned the passport. Tomlinson hurriedly slipped the nonsmoking Wilson another pack. 'Stick the fags up and you'll be through in seconds.'

'What?'

'Just do it.'

He did, and passed through. A man approached. 'Bob Tomlinson? Ross Wilson?'

'Yes.'

'My name is Pavel. Come with me to your hotel.'

They booked into the spectacular Cosmos Hotel, an enormous edifice constructed for the 1980 Olympic Games which had since sunk into a condition of graceless, uncomfortable torpor.

'Tomorrow,' said Pavel Tsarvoulonov in the vast echoing foyer of the Cosmos, 'you will see Madame Kolesnikova.'

'She will have answers for us?' asked Tomlinson wearily.

'She will see you tomorrow. I think you will find that she will help you.'

Too tired to sleep, and unable to escape the thousand questions in his mind, at three in the morning Bob Tomlinson got out of bed, put on his tracksuit, and went jogging through Moscow. Through clean parks and unthreatening streets he trotted, enjoying the last quiet hours of a safe and crime-free Russian capital, and two hours later he collapsed back into bed.

At 7.00 a.m. he woke to find that on that morning, it was the turn of the region of Moscow in which the Cosmos Hotel was situated to forgo hot water and thereby preserve the energy of the central pumping plant. Tomlinson and Wilson showered and shaved in an icy deluge, and set off to see Madame Kolesnikova.

I have been here before, thought Tomlinson, as he entered the office of Nataliya Kolesnikova, KGB colonel and senior justice adviser to the Union of Soviet Socialist Republics. The shabbily dressed man seated by the door, the magazines extolling junior volleyball championships in Volgograd . . . but rather than the Soviet Embassy in London, this was the office

of the state prosecutor of the entire Soviet Union, and rather
than Guennadi Shabannikov blinking genially from behind his
spectacles beyond the inner door, the two Scots were con-
fronted by uniformed military personnel – and by Nataliya
Kolesnikova.

Wilson and Tomlinson had enjoyed the usual, predictable
jokes about this senior official: surely a Rosa Klebb archetype,
built like a pocket battleship stuffed into a brass-bound uniform, sturdy shoes with poison tips, tight lips, piercing eyes,
and a larynx like sandpaper . . .

'This is Nataliya Kolesnikova,' said Pavel Tsarvoulonov,
and Tomlinson shook hands with one of the most charming
women he had ever met. With the grace and figure of a retired
ballet-dancer she rose to welcome them, smiling cheerfully.
This is a KGB colonel? thought Tomlinson, handing over the
gifts of perfume and a silk scarf which had, at the time of
purchase, seemed a little optimistic but were now, blessedly,
perfect.

The room was small, and they talked through Pavel
Tsarvoulonov. We are here simply as journalists, Tomlinson
stressed again, we have no religious or political axe to grind.
Make it clear to them that you will not be used, he told himself
constantly: you are nobody's stooge.

'What would happen to this Gecas,' asked Colonel Kolesnikova, 'if he was found guilty in your country?'

'Before we find him guilty we need the evidence.'

'We have all the evidence.'

'If you have the evidence, what do you want to happen?'

Kolesnikova replied immediately: 'We want him to return
to this country to stand trial here.'

'Britain does not have an extradition treaty with the
USSR.'

Kolesnikova nodded and smiled. 'You asked me what we
wanted,' she said. 'That is what we want.'

'Many people in Britain don't think he'll get a fair trial
here. We don't trust your judicial system.'

'He would get a fair trial here. You can go where you like and film what you like, you will see that. And we have the evidence.'

'There is another thing,' said Tomlinson. 'The British public, and I agree with them, has a revulsion against capital punishment. You will get no sympathy from Britain if it seems that you want somebody back in order to execute them.'

'Well . . . there is a problem. You have a system, and we have a system. But he must be put on trial.'

'This evidence . . .' said Tomlinson.

'In the next two weeks,' their host replied through the steady services of Pavel Tsarvoulonov, 'you will speak to eye-witnesses. You will see original documents. And,' she continued, 'I am going to advise my government to ask the British government to extradite Antanas Gecas to stand trial in the Soviet Union.' Then she stood, placed her hands on the table before her and said: 'Tomorrow we travel to Vilnius.'

'Where is Vilnius?'

'Lithuania.'

There were no aeroplane tickets in the old Soviet Union. People queued for flights as if they were catching a bus. When the jet taxied towards the terminal, would-be passengers scrambled, running towards its steps in a frantic effort to gain a seat. Fortunately, Aeroflot had retained seats for Madame Kolesnikova's guests, and as Tomlinson and Wilson made their way aboard other unlucky passengers were ejected. It was a converted military aircraft, with no cabin for the pilot. As a man in a mackintosh strolled past them up the aisle, Wilson joked: 'The pilot!' The man in the mackintosh duly sat down at the controls, flicked a switch, revved the engine into life and took off. A stewardess made her way up the aisle carrying 12 cups and a jug of water. Twelve people were given the cups; they drank and handed the cups back; the stewardess refilled them and passed them on to the next dozen. White knuckled and green faced, Ross Wilson sat back to enjoy his flight.

It was night-time when they arrived in Vilnius: it seemed to be night-time when they arrived anywhere in the Soviet Union; as if somebody had evolved an itinerary around perpetual evening. They booked into a hotel skirted by a wide, meandering river which was crossed by half a dozen bridges; a hotel which could and should have been acceptably picturesque, but which Tomlinson would, in the years ahead, come to hate with an unreasoning passion: the Hotel Lietuva. On the following day, in the company of the newly arrived Nataliya Kolesnikova, they went to the office of the Lithuanian chief prosecutor, a huge, bushy-eyebrowed bear of a man named Jurgis-Antanas Juozo Bacucionis. It was a short drive from the Hotel Lietuva to Bacucionis's office, or a 15-minute walk. By the same token that Bob Tomlinson could not guess, in the early March of 1987, how much he would come to detest the Lietuva, he was not to know that he would come to be as familiar with that 15-minute walk as with his own Glasgow driveway, come to know every paving slab, every traffic light, every cobble in the street.

They sat in his room beneath a picture of Lenin, and Bacucionis smoked endless Russian cigarettes through a worn holder, and Tomlinson asked again to see eye-witnesses.

'Tomorrow,' said Bacucionis affably, stubbing out a cigarette. 'Tomorrow you will see eye-witnesses. Migonis, Mickevicius and Aleksynas. If not tomorrow, the next day.'

'We don't have time to chop and change.'

'You will see them over the next two days.' The big man smiled, and pushed some documents towards them. 'These are from the trial of Jonas Plunge,' he said. Tomlinson and Wilson turned through the pages of the transcript of this war-crimes trial, and as Pavel Tsarvoulonov translated they looked at each grimly. There, again, was the name of Antanas Gecevicius, turning up as frequently as punctuation marks, implicated once more in a series of gruesome mass murders committed by the 12th Lithuanian Auxiliary Battalion.

'You know a lot about Gecevicius?' asked Tomlinson.

'We asked your country to investigate him ten years ago. We never so much as received a reply.'

Although Eli Rosenbaum had, while in Britain, mentioned the Plunge trial, and the fact that Gecas's name was cited there, Tomlinson had never seen any of the trial documents. For the first time, in that small town on the westerly outskirts of the Soviet Union, he was holding in his hands the record of a war-crimes trial, and it pulsed like electricity. This was, after all, what it all came down to: this was the kind of hearing which, if his investigations had any logical outcome, he was working towards. It was a thick wad, wrapped in a brown paper folder worn with age. Nothing could have been more different from the document which Tomlinson had brought with him as a tour guide: the three sheets of carefully hand-written paper that Neal Sher had taken away from Moston Terrace in 1982.

Yet by agreeing to and then signing Sher's short interview in 1982, Gecas had left a spoor. He named his starting point, Kaunas. He agreed being with the 2nd Battalion in Sanciai Barracks in Kaunas in the summer of 1941. He acknowledged that he had then moved to Minsk. He remembered 'going to the Slutsk area to fight'. He put his initials to being present at the shootings at the village of Dukara. He did all of this while under the impression that he was being asked to help to convict a former colleague, Lieutenant Jurgis Juodis, but he did it all the same . . . he must have felt so safe, thought Tomlinson, back then in 1982. He must have blithely assumed that nobody would ever follow the trail that he voluntarily left.

In Bacucionis's stark little cell of an office, against an imposing background smell of drains and stale dishwater, Tomlinson and Wilson first picked up the spoor. Between those damp walls, thick piles of confession and testimony first began to put flesh on the skeleton of Neal Sher's short and vital interview. As Pavel Tsarvoulonov's voice went on and on in translation of the documents, and as the name of Antanas Gecevicius recurred throughout the murderous career of Jonas

Plunge, it became evident that, even in his frankest, most engaging interviews back in Edinburgh, Mr Gecas had left quite a lot unsaid.

'So you did try to do something about Gecas, as a result of this trial?' Tomlinson asked Bacucionis.

'Yes. When we came across the name of Gecevicius we tried to track him down. But our first priority was to find those criminals still living in Lithuania, or elsewhere in the Soviet Union. Now, though, Gecevicius is very much a wanted man in the Republic of Lithuania.'

'If we return in three or four weeks' time with cameras, will you say that on film?'

Bacucionis nodded: the image of a Chicago police sergeant, thought Tomlinson. 'I will,' he said.

The two Scots returned to the grim delights of the Hotel Lietuva and placed a telephone call from the dimly lit reception to David Scott in Glasgow. Four hours later the call came through to their room, at about the time that Tomlinson's attempts to bribe the hotel staff with bars of soap and pairs of tights to make a samovar of tea were finally bearing fruit.

'How's things?' asked Scott.

'Wonderful. Just wonderful. We are about to drink an enormous quantity of champagne.'

They did make it to the Black Bar. There was a Black Bar in virtually every Soviet town, out of bounds to the local citizenry but open to foreigners and their hard Western currency. The Vilnius Black Bar was cold and nobody else was in it. In years to come it would be as crowded with journalists as any Fleet Street tavern, but that was too far away and beyond too many adventures, too many upheavals, for the two men to guess in 1987. Its stock would have been shameful in an east end Glasgow dive, but in Lithuania it was an Aladdin's cave of choice and exotic variety. It also, they would later learn, served edible food. They drank a bottle of extremely bad German beer and then they went to bed. It was a poor preparation for one

of the most moving and traumatic days that either of the two
men would ever experience.

Bacucionis had arranged for them to travel to Kaunas, that
ancient capital of Lithuania, ring-fenced with antique forts,
where Antanas Gecevicius had first embarked on his career
with the 2nd, soon to become the 12th, Lithuanian Auxiliary
Battalion. There, they were to interview two of Antanas
Gecevicius's former comrades-in-arms, Motiejus Pranas
Migonis and Leonas Juozas Mickevicius.

But it was along a long, flat desolate road to one of those
crumbling medieval forts surrounding Kaunas that the big,
black Zill limousines of Colonel Kolesnikova and Procurator
Bacucionis first delivered their visitors from Great Britain. The
Ninth Fort at Kaunas – they were all numbered rather than
named – looked instantly like a vision of Auschwitz or Dachau.
That was fitting. The Ninth Fort, like some of its fellows, had
been converted by the Germans in 1941 into a death camp and
had since been kept intact, in its state of devilish grace, by the
Soviet authorities.

The men entered through a small gate, a gate through
which thousands of Jewish men, women and children had
been herded in 1941. An atmosphere of dread and evil hung
like a vapour around the Ninth Fort at Kaunas, as though no
passing of the years, no piercing Baltic wind had succeeded in
dispersing the horror of what had been achieved there in the
summer and autumn of 1941. The vileness of it was as tangible
as the frozen earth on which they walked.

'Eighty thousand Jews,' Tomlinson and Wilson heard,
shuddering only partly from the cold, 'were marched into the
courtyard of the fort . . . here, and assembled . . . over there.
They were then forced up and out to the external wall . . .
here. Then they were shot.'

Machine-gun bullet holes pockmarked the walls like
smallpox. Where are the 80,000 buried? they asked their
guides.

'You are standing on their graves.'

In the window niches of the Ninth Fort had been inserted
stained-glass mosaics designed by Soviet artists as memorials
to the dead. And in the cells which acted as holding areas for
the newly arrived, as clearing-houses for the condemned,
names had been scratched on the walls – along with the city of
their author's origin: Nice, Paris, Hamburg . . . Jews from all
over Europe had been transported here, not to Poland or
Germany to be murdered, but also here, to the Soviet Union.

Standing in cells which would, 45 years ago, have been
packed solidly with terrified people awaiting the fate about
which they could no longer deceive themselves or their loved
ones – people from the great European diaspora and people
from just down the road in the Kaunas ghetto – Tomlinson
and Wilson were struck dumb. Bereft and appalled, they
looked silently about. Under one of the stained-glass windows
there lay on a plinth, lit by a single spotlight from above, a
small pyramid, about a foot in height, of human bones.
Tomlinson gave way to tears. 'I know,' said Wilson. 'I know
how you feel. Remember we're here to do a job. Let's just get
on with it.' As they left they passed two display cabinets
containing the tiny shoes which had been taken from Jewish
children. They would have fitted no child older than 12
months.

They ate a miserable lunch in an hotel in Kaunas, in a
dining-room containing 100 tables, only one of which was set,
and their party ate alone. It was 25°C below freezing both
inside and outside the building. Any of the usual interest in
foreign ways which can enliven the employment of journalists
abroad had disappeared, vanished in the miasma of the Ninth
Fort. Their minds were fully concentrated on the terrible work
that they had set themselves.

'Gecas and his battalion,' said Tomlinson to Bacucionis
and Kolesnikova, 'were they involved here?'

'We are not aware that they were. There is another fort –

the Seventh Fort – where Germans let Lithuanians do the killing. But we think not here, at the Ninth.'

Perversely, Tomlinson and Wilson found the answer pleasing. Talking to each other across the table in the broad Glasgow accents that even Pavel Tsarvoulonov could not decipher, they agreed that it showed a promising honesty on the part of their hosts. Had they wanted just to fit Gecas up before a couple of gullible – and at that moment profoundly susceptible – foreigners, they could have replied, yes, of course he was. It seemed that Scottish Television was not being fed false information.

Motiejus Pranas Migonis lived in a multi-storey high-rise block scheme similar to Drumchapel or Easterhouse, acre after acre of bleak urban despair, lacking in shops, bars, restaurants. A small man, 68 years old at the time, Migonis had already served a life sentence in Siberia for his part in the atrocities committed by the 2nd/12th Lithuanian Battalion. On the wall of his thankfully heated room there hung a single tapestry, a small flash of colour in the gloom.

Motiejus Migonis had been an ordinary soldier, a private. His war had consisted, he freely if not cheerfully agreed, almost entirely of executing Jewish civilians. And one of the areas in which Motiejus Migonis had operated, under his platoon commander, Lieutenant Antanas Gecevicius, was the small township of Slutsk in Byelorussia.

'That was the end of October 1941,' he told the company. 'Together with officers and soldiers of the 12th Battalion and some German soldiers – several thousand people were executed. At this place nearby (the town) were trenches, and I know that there were shootings at this place. Gecevicius was the officer.'

'Were you and Gecevicius by any chance involved at the Ninth Fort?' offered Tomlinson. The answer caused Bacucionis's bushy eyebrows to rise.

'Yes,' replied Migonis. 'And at the Seventh.'

In London Bob Tomlinson had asked Gerald Draper how a simple, untrained civilian journalist went about interviewing alleged war criminals. What line of questioning could you possibly take, to dredge the truth from this awful pit? 'You must ask them to be very precise,' Draper had replied. 'You must ask them, if they say they saw someone hold a weapon, how did they hold it? Did they hold it up in the air? Did they hold it straight out in front of them? Did they hold it pointed at the ground? Was it a rifle, or was it a pistol? How did they carry it? What was the order? Who was shooting? How far were they from their victims?. . .'

Knowing that the 12th Battalion had travelled from Lithuania to Minsk by motor convoy, Tomlinson put Migonis to the Draper test. 'When you got on the train to Byelorussia, did the officers travel in your compartment, or in another?'

'No, no, no.' Migonis shook his head emphatically. 'You've got it wrong. We travelled in lorries, in convoy. The officers were in the front, with the drivers, we were always in the back. We were never on a train.'

It was small, but it seemed important. Migonis not only remembered clearly, he was also prepared to correct his questioner.

'Can we film you saying this?'

Migonis nodded.

'Could we take you back to Slutsk, and film you there?'

He paused. 'Why not?' he said.

They were offered tea by his wife, which they declined, and said farewell to the cheerful, friendly old couple. It was difficult to believe that the last two hours had been spent in the company of a man who had served a life sentence for being involved in the mass murder of men, women and children. The 'quiet neighbour' front adopted by such people in fearful exile might not, after all, be such a difficult posture to adopt.

On the landing outside the flat Procurator Bacucionis pulled Tomlinson and Wilson to one side. 'I don't believe that he has just told you the truth,' he said.

Tomlinson chilled. 'Why? How?'

'You are the journalist, and it's up to you whether or not you believe him about this. But I don't believe that he was ever at the Ninth Fort. At the trials in which he has given evidence he has never previously mentioned the Ninth Fort. I think he is getting confused with the Seventh Fort. We will go there, later.'

Leonas Juozas Mickevicius lived on Lenin Avenue, a main street in the centre of Kaunas. He also had joined the 2nd Lithuanian Battalion at Sanciai Barracks in the early summer of 1941, when he was 26 years of age. He also had served 18 years' imprisonment in Siberia as a consequence. He, also, had travelled in those motor convoys . . .

'In the autumn of 1941,' he said, 'together with soldiers of [what had become] the 12th Battalion, I was taken to shoot Jews in the city of Kleck. Seven hundred Jews were taken to the central square of the town. The Jews were walked outside of the city, maybe one-and-a-half kilometres away. They were shot near a hill, where there had been dug a pit. I was on guard, and I saw how the Jews were laid in the pit, and soldiers following Gecevicius's command were shooting them with rifles. After the execution, Gecevicius and several other soldiers were checking who still remained alive.'

Tomlinson, still adopting the Draper formula, slipped in a description of Anatanas Gecas as small and dark haired.

'You've got the wrong man, then,' said Mickevicius. 'Gecevicius was a tall man, blond, very tall.'

There's no way these characters could have been rehearsed, Tomlinson and Wilson agreed. Central casting for the Royal Shakespeare Company couldn't have found them. They were true. And they were implicating Antanas Gecas and his battalion in far more than Scottish Television had ever dreamed.

'Okay,' said Tomlinson to Bacucionis, 'take us to the Seventh Fort.'

'We think that the Lithuanian Battalion was involved

here,' said Bacucionis as they approached the gaunt, isolated
medieval pile, 'but we have no solid evidence.' He looked
round at them. 'None that would stand up in our courts,
anyway.'

We are the first, thought Tomlinson, and that is why they
are being so careful. We are only journalists, but we are the
first investigators from the British Isles that these people have
received, the first to show an interest in crimes that have
monopolised the largest part of their professional lives. They
actually do want to get it right. They have entertained investigators from the governments and from the justice departments
of Canada and the United States and from 30 other countries,
but astonishingly – to us and to them – we are the first from
Britain.

The Seventh Fort was a crumbled hulk in the desolate
plain. It bore a plaque which commemorated the Jews murdered there. They stood and shivered in silent homage for no
longer than was decent, and then they turned and took the
long, straight highway back to Vilnius: a road without signs,
markings, or white lines that stretched as straight and unyield-
ing as a prairie railway-track across 80 miles of the broad,
monotonous Vilnya River basin. Nothing broke the landscape,
few vehicles other than horse-drawn carts shared the road.

'Would you like a beer?' asked Bacucionis through the
interpreter, halfway through this bucolic desert.

The Scots looked about, puzzled. 'Sure.'

The procurator told his driver to turn right. They drove
for half an hour through thickly forested flatlands and came at
last upon a modern hotel built in the Scandinavian style. It was
a hotel from the realms of fantasy: a hotel without guests,
containing a bar with no customers. Bacucionis ordered three
chilled beers, and Tomlinson felt suddenly sick. They drove
back to Vilnius in silence. Once back at the Hotel Lyatova, they
placed another call to David Scott, bartered for a samovar of
tea and cold meat sandwiches, and after four hours Wilson
and Tomlinson were able to tell Scott that they were about to

descend to the bar and consume several large bottles of champagne.

'What about the beer?' came the kindly inquiry from Glasgow.

'No. We don't fancy the beer at all. In fact, there is no beer.'

They sat and looked again at the three sheets of paper that Neal Sher had extracted from Antanas Gecas. It was like an orienteering marker. They could tick off Kaunas. In two days time they would be going to Minsk. If Gecas is guilty of these things, they agreed, he signed and initialled his own warrant back in 1982. Neal Sher of the United States Office of Special Investigations had stitched him up like a patchwork, and he had never felt a thing.

Breakfast at the Hotel Lietuva was a bubble-and-squeak from hell. Random assortments of vegetables and meats left over from previous days – from previous months – were fried up and served to the expectant guests with sliced bread and tea from two large samovars. The other diners were chiefly Georgian and Afghani labourers, and as Tomlinson and Wilson were routinely surrounded by their hosts from the KGB there was a minimum of cheerful badinage swapped across the table-tops. What fun there was to be had came from the fact that their fellow guests must assume that Tomlinson and Wilson also were from the KGB. In an attempt to bolster this illusion, Tomlinson loudly hummed the Soviet national anthem throughout the meal.

Then they broached the cold again, noted that it had begun to snow and wondered if this might not herald a slight improvement in the air temperature, and made in the convoy of Zill limousines for the village of Alytus and the third of Antanas Gecas's former colleagues, Juozas Janos Aleksynas.

Alytus was in a closed area. Nobody without official sanction could travel in its vicinity. After two hours they arrived and waited on the outskirts of town, where they were

met by police cars and another Zill limousine, and whisked to
the local procurator's office. There, waiting for them, was the
former sergeant of the 12th Lithuanian Battalion, Juozas
Aleksynas.

This man, with his knowledgeable eyes, his impish,
friendly grin and his handshake like a vice, had known
Antanas Gecevicius very well indeed. He had served ten years
in Siberia for their shared experiences. He was also disarmingly
willing to discuss the road that his and Gecevicius's life had
taken in 1941.

'I remember there were plenty of Jews killed in Minsk,'
he said. 'They were taken in a column to the place of mass
execution, four in a row. The execution there lasted for two
days, and I think there were thousands of people executed.
Groups of soldiers were filed up close to the pit. They were
commanded by officers. Our group was commanded by Gecevicius. He gave us orders: Attention! Fire! When we served
together in the battalion he was my direct commander. So I
think during these six months, or something like that, I knew
him quite well.'

'Is this all the truth? Has anybody told you to say this?'

Aleksynas's brow furrowed, and he barked back angrily:
'I am telling you the truth about what I am remembering. I am
not inventing anything.'

Back in the Hotel Lyatova, the emergency imported
rations of Jacobs biscuits, cheese slices and triangles, tinned
corned beef and salmon, tea bags and chocolate were running out. So Wilson and Tomlinson had a party with Pavel
Tsarvoulonov, breaking out a couple of bottles of duty-free
Scotch. David Scott's call was duly connected as the festivities
raged.

'Had any beer today?' he asked.

'No. We're about to have a magnum of champagne.'

'Is it really that good?'

'It's better than you'd ever believe. We're bringing it
home.'

Then they dined ravenously on corned beef and biscuits, sitting like shipwreck survivors on the bed, and then the three men got drunk.

The train from Vilnius to Minsk left on the following evening. Rather like the train which took Omar Sharif into exile in *Doctor Zhivago*, but missing some of that vehicle's basic amenities, it was a romantic, evocative journey. Tomlinson would learn later that an extra carriage had been appended to the train – a carriage at the back that he and Wilson knew nothing of – in which Colonel Kolesnikova travelled, as the Soviets called it, 'Soft Class'. The Scots went Hard Class, through the night across the endless steppes. Open coal fires burned at the end of each corridor, where passengers could smoke and where the conductor served tea brewed on the stove. They shared biscuits, cheese and chocolate with a young woman engineer in their compartment, and as she began to undress for bed they hurriedly escaped – to her surprise and hilarity – into the corridor; where, as the train hurtled towards Minsk, they finished off the whisky with the carriage conductor, and their conversation turned once again towards Neal Sher's signed statement of 1982 . . .

'There's no mistaken identity here.'

'No. He admits to both names.'

'He's signed for both names.'

'He's placed himself at Kaunas.'

'Where 80,000-plus Jews were murdered.'

'There's no direct evidence that he was involved in that.'

'He's placed himself in Minsk.'

'Plenty were murdered there.'

'And there's direct evidence that he was up to his armpits in it.'

'And he's placed himself in Slutsk.'

'Where witnesses say he commanded killings.'

The train pulled into Minsk in the middle of the night. And on the following day they were taken in another, smaller convoy of limousines to Slutsk.

'Many people in the town know that you are coming,' said the local Byelorussian procurator. 'I have told them so. And they all want to talk about the Lithuanians.'

They did. One old lady accompanied them to the killing fields outside the town, where a memorial to the dead stood among raised mounds of earth, crowded, mossy necropolises among the tall pines which stretched towards the lowering sky. 'I came out here after the killings,' she said.

'What . . . what did you find?'

'What did I find? I found dead bodies here, and my husband dead, and that was all. Nothing else.'

'How had your husband been murdered?'

She pulled her headscarf closer against the wind, and pursed her toothless gums. Her eyes looked blank and tired, but she spoke with strength, still motivated by the depth of former sorrows.

'From the rifle. Maybe from the revolver. One bullet was in his forehead, the other one in his neck. There were many people lying here. There were trenches with people lying in them here. But I was not looking around. I was just looking at my grief.'

Once back in Minsk, the two men were told of Maly Trostenets concentration camp, which had been built in 1942 by the forced labour of Jews and Russian prisoners-of-war, and which was the site of the murder of 250,000 people.

'Were the Lithuanians involved here?'

'We think so, but we cannot prove it.'

They visited an old man's house, behind a complex of hen-houses and chicken-wire, and were taken up to his attic where he showed them how he had watched the convoys of lorries arrive day after day, unloading their human cargo to dig their own mass graves before being shot and left to rot in the tangle of 10,000 lifeless limbs. 'And in the end there were a quarter of a million dead out there . . . and there were 260 such camps in the Republic of Byelorussia.'

The Minsk procurator, Georgy Yarnavskiy, felt strongly

that Antanas Gecas should be returned to his republic for trial, despite the fact that the case was being handled in Moscow and Vilnius. 'It was the people of Byelorussia who suffered. He should stand trial here.'

He spoke quietly and politely, but beneath his tone there was a hint of simmering discontent. It was not the first time that Tomlinson had detected this undercurrent. All of these Soviet professionals had been pleasant to an unexpected degree, all of them plainly eager to impress the first serious investigators from Britain – but in all of them, thinly disguised, was an anger at Tomlinson's country and Tomlinson's compatriots which occasionally came close to breaking the polite, professional veneer.

'Why has nothing been done about this man in your country?' the Minsk procurator would ask, his voice calm but his eyes urgent. And his unspoken conclusion was: You do not care. Your people and your government count ours for nothing . . . and his unacted wish was, it sometimes seemed, to pick up these two pleasant representatives of the British media by their lapels and shake them until their eyeballs bubbled and they saw the sense of making criminals answer for such wickedness as he had seen, as had been imposed upon the people of the Republic of Byelorussia.

'We hope that once the procedures have been completed, he can be extradited and we can put him on trial, here in the Soviet Union,' was all, in the end, that Yarnavskiy said, looking at Tomlinson and Wilson with an expression close to bewilderment.

Their grisly round of destroyed communities continued through Byelorussia, to Hatyn, where a gutted village had never been rebuilt, but left there on the plain as a maze of bare foundations beneath a single tolling bell. 'In the summer of 1943,' the official guide at Hatyn told them, 'the Nazis came to this village to ruin it. They killed 165 old people by burning them alive in this barn. They fed young children under the age of one year to their dogs to save on food. Like all of these villages, it is now dead . . .'

And as the atrocious tales mounted, each one more harrowing than the last, Tomlinson and Wilson felt their nerves – so frail just a few short days ago – begin to callous and harden. There is only so much that you can hear and digest and not, like Professor Gerald Draper, bend irrevocably beneath the weight of human evil. They became, and they remained, numb before the scale of what they were allowed to see of this forgotten holocaust.

At the Central Museum in Minsk they were taken to see photographs of hangings which had been carried out by the 12th Lithuanian Battalion under the command of Major Impulevicius: of young men with tears in their eyes looking helplessly for the last time around the streets of Minsk as Impulevicius carefully re-adjusted the noose at their necks, of women swaying lifelessly in the god-forsaken square. And there they were also shown Order Number 42, which gave any German soldier or any person acting on behalf of the German authorities the right to shoot a Jew at any time, without provocation, without suspicion of subversion, without the need for a command, without – in short – reason.

Minsk represented the end of the trail that Antanas Gecas had left to posterity, courtesy of Neal Sher and the US Department of Justice. He had not trodden that trail and merely seen 150 partisans executed at Dukara and a few shot at Slutsk. In the few summer and autumn months of 1941 in which Antanas Gecas had journeyed with his battalion from Kaunas to Slutsk, the plains became sodden with the blood of uncounted thousands of civilian Jews. That was the flesh on his skeletal account. He had a case to answer.

Bob Tomlinson and Ross Wilson moved south to the Ukraine, and the erstwhile haunts of the Beast of Borosov, Kyrylo Zvaritch, who had died in a Bolton hospital in 1984 despite years of effort on the part of his former neighbours to have him returned to face their courts. Zvaritch, they learned, had been a willing recruit to the auxiliary forces of the Third Reich after Operation Barbarossa. In a republic which lost five million people to the hands of the German invaders and their local allies, his activities had to be outstandingly brutal to live for long in the memory.

Tomlinson and Wilson were taken to the small village of Ture, which was within the aegis of Zvaritch's rule of terror. A christening party had taken place there one Christmas, at which the uninvited Zvaritch appeared. He sat down and promptly shot a guest in the head. The dead man's sister was introduced to Tomlinson . . . 'I came into the room, and Zvaritch asked me, who are you? And I said, I am his sister. And he said, if you are his sister you should bury him tomorrow. Not in the cemetery, but like a dog – '

The old woman shook with tears, and her daughter interrupted: 'My mother is quite old,' she said in a harsh peasant dialect which contrasted sharply with their interpreter's educated tones. 'She is 81, and already she forgets a lot of things. But I won't forget these things. I was ill at the time. I remember very well how I was playing with the girls in the village, and then people started rushing out of this house, crying. My uncle was shot. When we entered, Zvaritch was walking around the room. My uncle was sitting like this – ' she slumped to one side in her seat and let her head loll lifelessly upon her shoulder ' – and there was a stream of blood going on the floor.'

On the next day the family attempted to ignore Kyrylo Zvaritch's advice as to the murdered man's burial, and took his body to the local cemetery. 'Zvaritch was hiding in the bushes as a couple came to bury my uncle. He came out and killed them. First he killed the husband, shooting him in the back of the head, and then he shot the wife in the back. She was still alive. He came up to her, turned her over, and shot her in the head. My mother knew Zvaritch very well. They lived in the same village.'

What benefit could there be to the British government in protecting a man like that, a psychopathic killer let loose to satisfy his cravings by complicity with a bestial regime? What glorious cause was being served by refusing to answer petitions for his extradition? What honour to Great Britain, that he should dignify its soil with the last 40 years of his life?

That was not the sum total of Kyrylo Zvaritch's exploits. He had been guilty, his former neighbours claimed, of the random murder of some 140 people. He had burned alive a wedding party inside a barn. He had taken babies from their mothers, held them by the legs, and shot them dead. He had . . . enough. Too much. It was Ross Wilson's turn to be affected by this single tragedy. Where Tomlinson had broken beneath the enormity of the Ninth Fort at Kaunas, the director wept at the microcosmic atrocity at Ture.

'We're here to do a job, remember?'

Wilson nodded, and they prepared to leave for Moscow, and Great Britain.

6

'David, we have to go back. We can prove the case. We can't not pursue it.' They were sitting in Scott's room on the Monday morning after their return to Scotland. Outside the window the ordinary world of western civilisation went about its daily business.

Scott needed little convincing. It would require a month's filming, which is a considerable financial commitment for a television company, and it meant operating in a country where the Western media had never previously been made welcome, but Scott had decided before the two men returned that if they could answer a minimum of questions satisfactorily, they would be refuelled and turned round with a TV crew on their backs.

'Do you have enough eye-witnesses?'

'Oh, yes.' The two men named them. Aleksynas, Mickevicius, the villagers of Ture . . . it seemed a universe away, a century away.

They ran through the additional venues in which Antanas Gecas had performed during 1941. They told Scott of the trials in which he had been cited, time and again, as an accessory to genocide. They told of the leads to be followed up, and of the extraordinary fertility of this untested region. They sat and talked into the night throughout Monday and Tuesday.

'We have to get back there quickly. American TV stations are on to it, they're trying to get access.'

At 7.30 on the Wednesday morning Tomlinson arrived at work to find a summons from Scott.

'What are you doing at the weekend?'

Expecting a convivial night with David and Liz Scott, the journalist happily replied that he and Maggie were free.

'In that case, get back to Russia and get this in the can.'

Tomlinson caught up with Wilson in a corridor. 'It's on!' he shouted. 'We're going.' They shook hands gleefully.

Four days later, days spent fielding questions from around the world – 'Is that Bob Tomlinson the Nazi-hunter?' 'No, it's Bob Tomlinson the journalist' – telephoning Shabannikov, telephoning Gerald Draper ('We have the evidence,' said Tomlinson to this sage. 'No, Mr Tomlinson,' replied Draper, 'you have the information. It will only become evidence once it is read in court. And that is going to be the battle.') – they were on a flight back to Moscow with a television crew and a different set of nerves. No longer the wracking fear of defeat, the dread of the story not standing up; simply now a niggling concern that witnesses might withdraw or documents go missing, that the film crew might be denied access, that Scottish Television might waste a large amount of money – a different, and marginally preferable baggage of concerns. Their brief was simple: to record the case against Antanas Gecas for involvement in war crimes; and the case against the British government for – at best – negligence, and at worst for the deliberate and cynical concealment of such men and their criminal past.

The crew was a good one: cameraman Kelvin Gray, assistant cameraman Walter MacGill, production assistant June Robin, electrician George Muir, soundman Clive Woods, director Wilson, and Tomlinson. In the month that was to follow, filming the bargain-basement of human depravity in awkward and uncomfortable circumstances, they held together well; answering depression and frustration with mutual support rather than argument. For that much, each of them would be profoundly grateful to the others before the month was out.

Because no matter how much the rest of the crew had been warned by Tomlinson and Wilson of what they were about to see, no warning could properly anticipate the effect of the Ninth Fort at Kaunas, or the archive photographs of mass hangings in Minsk, or the voice of a single, old, tired woman describing how her brother had his brains blown out at a christening party in his home village.

They flew into the dank and soulless abyss of Moscow Airport for the second time in three weeks, reflecting on how much more pleasant it had been, just seven days earlier, to fly out of it. Leaving the British Airways flight behind was, for Tomlinson and Wilson, an unnaturally poignant experience. They were disembarking from more than an aeroplane; they were going from the world of ample hot water and tea with sugar, to the world where such things were a matter of chance and barter.

On the first morning of shooting Tomlinson took eight takes to present a short speech to camera. In the thrill of the chase, he realised, he had lost some basic discipline. He had taken his eye off the ball and neglected the essentials of documentary work: the links, the script, the routine journalism. It was time to remember again that Scottish Television were in the Soviet Union to prepare a piece of journalism.

They interviewed Nataliya Kolesnikova in Moscow. 'Shall I wear my uniform?' she asked.

'No, no . . .' how to phrase it? 'Madame Kolesnikova, you are a colonel in the KGB, and speaking frankly, the KGB does not have a good image in the Western world. Also, you look just fine as you are.'

'We on our part have a list of 34 war criminals in the territory of Great Britain,' she said. 'We could have co-ordinated and could have worked together on the issue, as we are doing with Germany, the United States, Austria, Canada and 30 other countries. Unfortunately, we have had no help from Great Britain . . . for some reason the British side does not want to solve the problem positively.'

They moved on from Moscow to Lithuania, to the Ninth Fort, to Mickevicius, Migonis and Aleksynas, and to the Hotel Lietuva. Procurator Bacucionis dispelled the last of the anxiety that had haunted Wilson and Tomlinson: the fear that the Soviet authorities might renege on their earlier promise. They felt an immediate comfort in the presence of that big, decent man, greeting them warmly and instantly displaying on his desk the crucial documents. It went some way towards easing the annoyance of finding, suddenly, a second interpreter – unannounced – in their company.

'Who's he?' Tomlinson asked Tsarvoulonov of this shadowy figure.

'Well,' replied Pavel, '. . . he's here. He's from Intourist. His name's Misha.' Misha was, without doubt, there to keep a careful eye upon the foreigners, and possibly also upon Pavel Tsarvoulonov, who was pleased to make it clear that he was not a member of the Communist Party.

That night, back in the Hotel Lietuva, Tomlinson asked Tsarvoulonov why he was not a Party member. 'I've never really got round to it,' the interpreter shrugged. 'And I don't see why I should. But I'm beginning to think that it's holding my career back. I'm working twice as hard as other guys for the same money.' Things would change in Tsarvoulonov's Russia. Within five years, he would be head of television services under the post-communist government of Boris Yeltsin.

They had visited the Ninth Fort that day, and a small, innocuous incident there would perturb Tomlinson's sleep for years to come, as a gentle, insinuating nightmare. It would never wake him, never have him upright in bed sweating and silently screaming, but it persisted like a rheumatism or an old wound, agitating itself into his fretful subconscious. Clive Woods, the soundman, was walking on the perimeter walls of the fort when he shouted to Ross Wilson to get a picture of a lamp that hung from an old guard tower. It had been there since 1941. A circular shade of gunmetal green hanging by a hook, it overlooked the cobbled Path of Death up which the victims had stumbled to their deaths at dawn and at twilight, and the wind that blew ceaselessly over the plain echoed faintly in the hollow lamp, and it creaked monotonously, insistently, as it must have creaked every minute of every day since the summer of 1941. The crew went silent as Ross Wilson filmed it and Clive Woods recorded the slow, obscure sound of metal rubbing against metal, like the ticking of an arthritic clock, as the lamp swayed slowly to and fro. For years, Bob Tomlinson could not rid his mind of that image and that noise. It came to him like a spectre in the watches of the night, not fierce or harmful, but a strange and persistent reminder.

On that same evening the crew mutinied, not at the subject matter they were obliged to cover (the trauma of the Ninth Fort was answered by a democratic decision, taken almost in silence, to seek out the Black Bar and drink it dry), nor at the unrequested presence of an Intourist KGB minder, but at the Hotel Lietuva's cuisine.

'There is a restaurant in Vilnius,' offered Pavel Tsarvoulonov. 'I will telephone, and make sure they have food.' Leaving the translator behind with a sore head and assurances that they could get by in English for one night at least, the team set off to eat out.

A group of students sat drinking in the main area of the restaurant. The Scots were taken into a back room, where they discovered that none of the staff spoke English. 'No problem,' said Clive Woods. 'We'll draw what we want to eat.' Carefully they drafted sketches of a pig and potatoes. The pig was then artistically filleted, and the potatoes chipped, and the drawings handed over to intelligently nodding staff. In due course seven plates appeared from the kitchen and were placed before the guests. They each contained nothing but sliced tomatoes. The crew ate their tomatoes and returned to the Hotel Lietuva to break open the corned beef and biscuits.

A Lithuanian interpreter had joined their party in Vilnius, and as they journeyed back in the minibus from filming at Panaray, past fields littered with giant hoardings exhorting the workers to produce more from the fields for their society ('In Ayrshire, it'd just say: "Dig, you bastards, dig",' came a voice from the back of the bus), past anti-aircraft gun emplacements littering the countryside like thistles, they noticed that this young woman was sitting with tears streaming down her face.

'Pavel, what's the matter with Vilty?'

'She's touched by you all. You're so nice, so hard working, so relaxed together.'

'Well, tell her we think she's a nice person, and all the people we've met have been helpful and co-operative.'

Vilty turned round from the front of the bus and said: 'Yes, but you are free. And I am not, and neither are my people.'

There was a stunned silence, instinct with the awful comprehension that Soviet citizens did not say such things to visitors in the Soviet Union – particularly when those visitors were representatives of a national television network, and the Soviet citizen in question was employed to translate for them the Lithuanian language. Was she for real? Was it – terrible thought – a set-up? Or were those tears and that drastic comment genuine? At least Misha wasn't in the bus.

'Among us,' ventured Tomlinson, 'you're free.' It seemed scant compensation.

A wedding party was taking place in the Soviet section of the Hotel Lietuva on the first Friday night of this visit, and the crew wandered down to witness the celebrations. Young dancers with aspirations to the Bolshoi were performing a high-quality cabaret. Red Army soldiers in uniform danced with each other to Bruce Springsteen's 'Born In The USA'. 'There's the answer to World War Three, Pavel,' the Scot observed. 'When your tanks come rolling in, we'll just play music. It'll be a Technical Knock Out. They'll just start dancing with each other. The only question left will be, who's won most points for artistic impression?'

Pavel appreciated the joke. Misha did not. 'Don't your soldiers like to dance?'

No comment. Let's not fall out over this.

They loaded their aluminium equipment cases on to the night train from Vilnius to Byelorussia, under the watchful eyes of soldiers pacing about in the gloom, and once again the Zhivago express set off east. There was an extra carriage attached on this occasion, but it was not Soft Class for KGB colonels. It was, to their delighted surprise, a buffet and dining car. Their joy was short lived – it lasted for as long as it took to see a dirty knife cut cheese, and then bread, and then meat. Even the chocolate was inedible. All of the crew had stomach upsets which not even the patent medicines dished out by their hosts could quell.

They arrived in Minsk and were bustled off to a hotel. One by one they disappeared into their rooms, and one by one they re-emerged in the corridor.

'Do you have a problem with your room?'

'Aye, I do.'

'I don't have a toilet seat.'

'Neither do I.'

'Nor me.'

'Mm.'

Led by Tomlinson and Pavel Tsarvoulonov, they all went down to reception and approached the manager.

'Toilet seats.' he said. 'We need up to a dozen toilet seats.'

'But you've got toilets.'

'Yes. But we need toilet seats.'

They followed the manager to his office, in which stood a huge grey filing cabinet, six feet in height and four feet square. The manager turned round in front of it.

'You definitely said toilet seats?'

'Yes. We definitely said toilet seats.'

The manager opened the filing cabinet. In the bottom corner, occupying two square feet of the vast storage area, were toilet seats in cellophane wrappers. The rest of the cupboard was filled, from wall to wall, floor to ceiling, with Tennents lager. The lager was past its drink-by date. To a

Scottish film crew in Minsk, however, that was a puny irrelev-
ance. They stood in silence, gazing with religious awe at the
big, grey filing cabinet. Fate had led them there. The inevitable
transaction was accomplished almost in a trance. 'Here's 20
dollars for the beer. We'll come back for the toilet seats.'

They were taken on a guided tour of the historical communist sights of Minsk – Lenin's secret meeting place, the
houses of important party members – and one by one the crew
slipped away, leaving Tomlinson alone, diligently responding
to their enthusiastic guide. And then they went, with the
cameras, to Slutsk.

An old man was standing in a field by the site of the
massacre. As the crew approached he began to shout. 'He
wants you to go and speak to him,' said Pavel Tsarvoulonov.
That was nothing new in Slutsk: at times it seemed that half
the town had first-hand accounts of what had happened when
the 12th Lithuanian Battalion arrived in October 1941; stories
of those terrible men in unusually coloured uniforms, speaking
an unfamiliar language, who killed for their German masters.
'He wants to tell you about the day they arrived,' said
Tsarvoulonov.

Tomlinson walked over the field towards the old man. He
wore a row of medals on the breast of his tattered suit.

'This is where they came in,' he said. 'I was standing
here. This is where you must film. This is where we fought.'

'It's not important to us to film here,' said Tomlinson to
Tsarvoulonov. 'Tell him, if we've got time . . .'

They walked back into the town, and from the outlying
streets the old man was still visible in his field. People
approached them from the doors of houses and began to
embrace the Scots, throwing their arms around the surprised
visitors and kissing them on the cheek. We're not the liberating
army, thought Tomlinson. This is a stitch-up, there's something phoney going on.

'Pavel, what's going on? What's this about? This is stupid,
they don't know me from Ronald Reagan.'

'They have heard that you are here investigating the conduct of the Lithuanians. Almost all of these people lost somebody.'

Tomlinson felt a pitiful sadness. Out in the fields, the old man was still standing against the blank horizon. My God, he thought, what have these people been through?

'I jumped over this wall – ' Tsarvoulonov was translating the words of another man in the street ' – I ran over there, I hid behind that small plot . . .'

It would be many years before Bob Tomlinson fully understood the response of the people of Slutsk to the presence in their town of a Scottish television crew. When he did, he was standing in an Edinburgh courtroom hearing the evidence of a single woman survivor, and he thought, with a pull of emotion, of that old man and his medals, alone in the field where they resisted the German advance.

Wilson and Tomlinson had decided before leaving Scotland not to tell the crew much about their reconnaissance mission. If they experienced the trauma themselves, without forewarning, the two men reasoned, then a professional crew would quickly reflect it in their own work. At the murdered village of Hatyn, its unpeopled stillness broken only by the single bell tolling for the dead, cameraman and sound technician alike responded to their feelings, and an emotional intensity charged their efforts. The sombre bass note of the bell at Hatyn and the clear, respectful images of the sculpted Roman numerals which signified the number of people destroyed there, the sunlight shafting through the tall pine forests, and beyond the wide and empty plains; those sounds and images would form the arresting cornerstone of this documentary film.

Another wedding was underway at the Black Bar in Minsk. George Muir took out his bagpipes at the request of the bride and groom and Tomlinson was urged to recreate the sword-dance that he had last performed at primary school. They came as a welcome relief, those moments of fun and half-intoxicated farce. In the morning, at their shoulder, there was always another killing field.

As they left Minsk, the crew knew that they had completed the Gecas story. They had the information which, surely, a Scottish court could not refuse as evidence. They had – in the can – testimony from eye-witnesses, from survivors, from fellow-collaborators, documentary evidence, court references, court reports. This was no hearsay but solid information. 'It will only become evidence once it is read in court,' Professor Draper had said. Well, that was not up to a television crew from Glasgow.

They travelled to Lvov in the Ukraine and filmed the legacy of the psychopath Kyrylo Zvaritch. They returned to Moscow and filmed Nataliya Kolesnikova again saying that the Soviet Union would be asking for the extradition of Antanas Gecevicius for trial in the country of his alleged crimes. That request would be received by the British government in August 1987, and it would be rejected out of hand.

It was left to Tomlinson to perform a final grisly duty, while the crew was collecting linking shots in the streets of Moscow. He went into the belly of the Soviet archives and extracted still and moving photographs of the holocaust. For eight hours he sat almost alone in a darkened room in a building the size of Waverley Station and watched mass graves being opened and dismembered, mutilated bodies being disinterred. A hundred reels of the pornography of war flickered past. At seven in the evening he was able to say, that is enough, these shots will do; and feeling miserably, physically sick he wandered out before the closing gates into the dull streets of Moscow on a cold March night.

'The good guys always win in the end,' he had made a habit of telling one procurator after another, throughout the Soviet Union, as they had wished him luck. They would shrug their shoulders, as much as to say: 'It's a nice sentiment, but . . .'

The Soviet media, locally and nationally, had taken an

interest in the work of this travelling film crew, and Wilson and Tomlinson found themselves regularly on the wrong side of the desk: giving press conferences to journalists in Vilnius, Minsk and Moscow. One or two questions recurred: 'Why have the British never shown any interest in this matter before?' 'Why did the British bomb Dresden?'. . . questions which the two men felt themselves to be incapable of answering. 'Why has Britain not done more?' came commonly from the floor. Already irritated by the universal Soviet insistence on referring to the 'Great Patriotic War', Tomlinson took to replying: 'We were fighting Fascism from 1939. Why did it take you until 1941 to join in?'

At one such gathering of about a hundred journalists, the query was put: 'What do you think of the Soviet Union?'

'The Soviet Union has two big enemies,' said Tomlinson. The Soviets looked up, pens poised. 'And they are Intourist and Aeroflot. They're more likely to damage your country than anyone from the outside.'

Throughout the long, sad journey, from village to town to massacred hamlet, where people had approached with further lists of killing, with stories of atrocity that piled into a gross, unmanagable mountain of death, it had become clear that the tragedy which had overtaken these republics between 1941 and 1945 could not be encompassed – not in an hour-long documentary, not in a month, not in a lifetime. Village representatives would hand over 150-name petitions, requesting from them – a film crew – the return of some murderer presently drawing a British pension. Could they track this person down? Could they ship him back?

And the certainty was always there, that old certainty that this would end in tragedy for someone, along with a doubt that overshadowed flippant bonhomie – did the good guys always win in the end? Or had the bad guys, in a very material sense, already enjoyed their victory?

Before leaving Britain, Tomlinson and Wilson had heard that Prime Minister Margaret Thatcher would also be visiting

Moscow that spring, and that she would give a press conference there. 'Pavel,' said Tomlinson to Tsarvoulonov one day.
'See Thatcher's visit – could you arrange for a Soviet journalist
to ask her a question? Ask her what she's going to do about
alleged war criminals living in her country? And make sure
there's a camera on her reply.'

It was done. At the end of March 1987, Margaret Thatcher
faced the international media in Moscow. A Soviet journalist –
whom Tomlinson would never meet – stood and, while the
cameras rolled, asked her about war criminals resident in
Britain . . .

The Iron Lady leaned purposefully towards the microphones. 'Well first,' she said, 'we have no effective extradition
treaty with the Soviet Union. Secondly, we have a list of
names.' Enunciating slowly, in a maternal, bedside manner,
she went on: 'We do not have evidence, strict evidence against
those names. Any question of extradition could only arise on
the basis of evidence, and not on accusation.'

It was a coup, an undoubted coup. The fact of an absence
of extradition arrangements with the Soviet Union was incon-
trovertible, even if it did not explain away the British refusal to
act against these men on its own behalf. But if Margaret
Thatcher only required evidence of wrongdoing . . .

Leaving Moscow Airport and boarding a British aircraft was as
sublime an experience as they had anticipated. They walked
into the terminal and passed a man reading a newspaper. He
let it fall from before his face and said: 'Ross Wilson? Bob
Tomlinson?'

'Yes? Why?'

He lifted the newspaper again.

'Do you know us?'

'No, no. It's okay.' He walked away.

They offered their remaining bags of tins of salmon,
biscuits and Scottish Television T-shirts to Pavel and Misha.
The latter refused. Boris Yeltsin's future head of television,

The two lives of Antanas Gecevicius and Antony Gecas: as a soldier decorated by the Reich; and as the quiet neighbour in Edinburgh, 50 years later (© Scotsman Publications)

Under orders:
Junior Lieutenant Gecevicius and his battalion are sent to the killing fields of Byelorussia. The Lithuanian commands read: 'The officers listed below left for the Minsk–Borosov–Slutsk areas on 6 October at 0500 hours.'

The monthly report of the Wehrmacht Commander in 'Ostland', dated 10 November 1941. The last sentence reads: 'During a purge in the area Slutsk–Kleck by Reserve Police Battalion 11, 5,900 Jews were shot.'

The Seventh Fort at Kaunas, scene of the murder of untold numbers of Lithuanian Jews

The hangings at Minsk, in the autumn of 1941. The Germans had a grisly fondness of recording such actions for their own amusement

The memorial at Slutsk

Bob Tomlinson: 'I am not a communist and I am not a Jew. I just want to get to the bottom of all this.'

David Scott: a resolute defender of his journalists

Peter Watson: a case which had to be won

Outside the courthouse during the first war-crimes trial to take place in Great Britain (© Scotsman Publications)

Daily Express 19/2/92

Nazi troops in 'conveyor belt' deaths

EXPRESS REPORTER

...AZI death squads ...arried out a two-day ...conveyor belt" opera- ...on to execute hun- ...reds of prisoners, a ...court heard yesterday.

Eduardas Goga, 78, told ...he Court of Session in ...Edinburgh that he was present when Russian PoWs and civilians were taken from a camp near Minsk in 1941 and shot.

Mr Goga, a retired farmer, said he was an NCO in a battalion formed to maintain public order in Lithuania after the German invasion.

He claimed that he ...saw sub-lieutenant...

WITNESS: Eduardas Goga

the mass graves to finish off the wounded.

Yesterday Mr Goga told the court: "This operation went on like a conveyor belt. Groups would be ...

DENIALS: Anton Gecas

17 alleged war criminals living in Britain. One was said to live in Edinburgh.

Mr Tomlinson, a former Journalist of the Year, told the court that he obtained from Israel the ...of Anton Gecas and

CONVEYOR BELT SLAUGHTER

Gecas court told of death squad

NAZI death squad slaughtered 10,000 ...sian prisoners, it was ...ned yesterday.

Court of Session was told ...rrific operation was like a ...r conveyor belt.

78-year-old Edvardas Goga court that alleged war crimi-

By GORDON McILWRAITH

nal Antony Gecas was one of the officers in the death squad.

Gecas, of Moston Terrace, Newington, Edinburgh, is claiming he was defamed in a documentary, Crimes of War. He is demanding £600,000 damages.

Goga, who had been flown to Edinburgh from Lithuania to give evidence for Scottish Television, said the incident took place in 1941 while he was serving in a Lithuanian battalion formed by the Nazis.

Goga said soldiers and officers took part in the slaughter. But he said he couldn't be sure that every officer had fired.

STV journalist Bob Tomlinson, 49, who investigated Gecas, said he first got on to the

GECAS ... officer

story after reading a Daily Record article in October 1986.

It had said that Nazi-hunters had produced a list of alleged war criminals in Britain, one of them in Edinburgh.

He obtained Gecas's name from Israel, looked him up in the phone directory and went to interview him.

The hearing continues.

Gecas 'was at slaughter pits'

Witness tells of massacre of 10,000 PoWs

By Alan Hutchison
Chief Reporter

HORRIFIC details of a two-day massacre of 10,000 Soviet prisoners of war by German and Lithuanian officers and soldiers during the Second World War were graphically outlined in the Court of Session in Edinburgh yesterday by a 78-year-old former Lithuanian soldier.

A historic war crimes defamation action, which began in Lithuania last week, resumed in Scotland in dramatic fashion with a former member of the German-led 12th Lithuanian [...]
Edvardas [...] slaught[...]
Byelorus[...] said ha[...]
belt.

Mr G[...] said tha[...]tony G[...]burgh, [...]

£600,000 defamation action against Scottish Television after it screened a documentary claiming that he had been a war criminal — had been among the group of Lithuanian and German officers at the pits. He said they had pistols in their hands.

He told the court that the soldiers, who were armed with rifles, and the officers were shooting at the same time. But later, under [...]

He said that hundreds of thousands of Lithuanians were deported and he described one incident where 70,000 civilians including doctors, students and priests were killed by Cheka officers "in the most cruel fashion".

Mr Goga, claiming that after the war he had been persecuted by the KGB for 30 years, said that in 1946 he had been sentenced to ten years in prison for "political partisan activities".

He described how he joined the Second Self Defence Battalion — later renamed the 12th Battalion — in July 1941 after the German invasion of his country. He explained that Lithuania had been under Soviet occupation and that the Germans were regarded as rescuers.

Questioned by Colin Campbell, QC, for Scottish Television, about his battalion's move to a prisoner of war camp near Minsk in October 1941, Mr Goga said he witnessed a very frightening sight.

Mr Goga, who had been a junior NCO, said that the prisoners, who were in Russian military uniforms, looked hardly alive. "They could hardly move," he added.

He said there were also a number of "Bolshevik activists" in the camp. And he went on: "We were told there were close to 10,000 people in the camp." Asked by Mr Campbell what had happened to the people in the camp after the battalion and the Germans arrived, he said: "The people at the camp were condemned to extermination, to be shot at pits about one kilometre away."

Mr Goga pointed out that the Germans were in charge of the whole operation and described how the Lithuanian soldiers formed a corridor between the camp and the pits.

"The prisoners would be taken by the Germans in groups of about 120. They would have to leave their clothes at the pits. They were driven to the pits and were shot there."

Mr Campbell: "Who was doing the shooting?"

Mr Goga: "Both [...] and German took [...] shooting."

Asked if Mr Geca[...]

others standing at the e[...] the pits. The officer[...] pistols in their hands. [...] not see exactly as the[...] their backs to us as they [...] at the edge of the pits."

Mr Goga confirmed th[...] Gecas had been one [...] officers present and sai[...] the prisoners were sho[...] groups. He declared: [...] operation went on like [...] veyor belt. Groups wo[...] taken in succession."

Cross-examined by D[...] Robertson, QC, for Mr G[...] about the incident [...] Minsk, Mr Goga was [...] whether he had been at[...] see from where he was s[...] ing whether every office[...] fired his pistol, or only [...] of them.

Goga .. watched killings

Edvardas Goga outside the Court of Session yesterday

present at the operation, he said: "Yes, he was there."

Mr Campbell: "What was he doing during the shooting?"

I would [...]
everyone [...]

before [...]
ues today[...]

Pictu[...]

80,[...]
in 'u[...]
ho[...]
at [...]

Jenny Shield[...]

death can[...]
role in a S[...]

VAST CONCRET[...] punch the sky and [...] maces, echo the last [...] of the prisoners who [...] ied here beneath a [...] plain.

In this chill landsca[...] tors pause only long er[...] read the simple insc[...] beneath this enc[...] memorial to victims [...] Nazis before hurrying [...]

This is the ninth [...] Kaunas in central Li[...] which was built on the [...] of Tsar Nicholas 11 in 1[...]

Originally construc[...] guard the strategically [...] town which stands at t[...] fluence of the Neris a[...] munas rivers, it was the[...] of innumerable atrocit[...] ing the Second World [...] when more than 80,000 [...] were massacred by the Ger[...] mans and their collaborators.

The tragedy of Jews in the Baltic states was graphically outlined in the 1989 report of the War Crimes Inquiry by Sir Thomas Hetherington and William Chalmers.

Between June and November 1941 more than 170,000 Jews were killed in Lithuania, about 70,000 in Latvia and almost all of Estonia's 1,000 Jewish population was wiped out.

According to the report: "At first the local population, encouraged by the German mobile killing squads, engaged in the killing and destruction of Jewish properties.

The most active were the Lithuanians who, according to German reports, killed some 3,800 Jews in Kaunas and 1,200 in other towns.

"From August until December 1941, under German civilian rule, the Einsatzgruppen, together with their local helpers, killed about 150,000 Lithuanian and most Latvian Jews.

"To help them in these mass killings, the Einsatzgruppen recruited auxiliary police. In Lithuania, anti-Soviet partisans were first encouraged to organise the "spontaneous" pogroms and then were dis-

'Nazis blasted POWs in pit'

AN old soldier told a Scots court yesterday how hundreds of Russian POWs were shot by Nazi death squads.

Eduardas Goga, 78, described how the killings continued for two days at a camp near Minsk in 1941.

Mr Goga, a member of a Lithuanian battalion, said he saw Antanas Gecevicius, a [...] ghetto in Kaunas and others transported hundreds of miles from other countries under German occupation — were among those shot.

In the labyrinthine cells and dormitories, which remain untouched to this day, can be read the farewell messages French prisoners scratched on the walls.

The Hetherington-Chalmers war crimes inquiry says there were "very few accounts" of help being offered to the Jews by the Baltic peoples but one cell in the ninth fort, which has been dedicated as a Jewish memorial, contains a photograph of the mother of the Lithuanian President Vitautas Landsbergis who is credited with sheltering Jews from the Nazis.

Tomorrow morning in the Court of Session in Edinburgh a war crimes defamation action opens before Lord Milligan.

The action has been brought by Mr Anton Gecas, a 75-year old Lithuanian-born Briton against Scottish Television which claimed, in a 1987 documentary, that he was a member of a Lithuanian police battalion under German command and committed war crimes in Lithuania and Byelorussia during the Second World War.

The television company is

The way of death: monument to the victi[...]

defending the action on the grounds that what was broadcast was true.

Last week, in an unprecedented legal move, Lord Milligan travelled to the Lithuanian capital of Vilnius to take evidence on commission from three witnesses in the case.

Two of them, J[...] synas and Motie[...] — both former [...] the 12th Lithua[...] battalion which w[...] Kaunas shortly a[...] man occupation [...] mer of 1941 — t[...] ing that Mr Gec[...]

Court hears of two-day killing orgy

TEN thousand captive Russians and Bolsheviks were shot dead in two days by Germans and Lithuanians in October, 1941, a witness told the Court of Session in Edinburgh yesterday.

Some were so ill they were barely able to move, said retired Lithuanian farmer Mr Edwardas Goga (78), then serving in a Lithuanian battalion whose task was to root out Bolsheviks.

He stood guard nearby as groups of 100-200 prisoners were marched from a German prison camp near Minsk to pits where they were stripped naked and shot.

Mr Goga was giving evidence in the case in which Antony Gecas (75), formerly known as Antanas Gecivicius, is suing Scottish Television for £600,000 over claims that he took part in the mass killing of civilians. Mr Gecas was not in court yesterday.

Speaking through an interpreter, Mr Goga told why he had joined up. "We were under Soviet occupation and when the Germans declared war and invaded the Soviet Union, we felt that they came as rescuers."

'Extermination'

He feared the Russians were prepared to annihilate the Lithuanian people.

Mr Goga said most of the prisoners in the camp were Russians in uniform, but there were also some civilians and Bolshevik activists.

Asked if he saw them [...] Mr [...]

centre[...]
expecte[...]
nore [...]
nclud[...]
ians. [...]
"The [...]
of th[...]
party' [...]
to fea[...]
forthe[...]

however, accepted the gifts graciously – 'and I will convince Misha that he is committing no sin by taking these things'. They then said their farewells, with the emotion of people who believe that they will never meet again.

'Could you ask the captain,' said Wilson to the purser, 'to tell us when we're out of Soviet airspace?' The announcement was greeted like a Scottish goal at Hampden.

The hour-long documentary *Crimes of War* went out on 22 July 1987. Professor Gerald Draper was interviewed in London, to add his authoritative passion to the exhibition of old newsreel, damning documentation, interviews with survivors, witnesses, Soviet procurators and KGB colonels displayed on screen. And once again, Draper stole the show.

'Say the commandant of Auschwitz, Rudolph Hoess,' posited the old man, 'who was commandant of Auschwitz–Birkenau, where they probably got rid of, by gassing alone – I'm not talking about petrol injections, hanging, flogging, starvation – they probably got rid by gassing alone of more than four-and-a-half million according to the records available. If that man had appeared in Great Britain tomorrow, and there was evidence available in shoals, we could have done nothing. We have not legislated for the trial of German war criminals, or indeed Japanese war criminals, in the United Kingdom. Not one single German war criminal, or for that matter Japanese war criminal, was tried in the United Kingdom.

'It has always been suggested that demands from the Soviet Union were not really demands to bring a war criminal to justice. The standard answer, which I think is a bit outdated, was, oh, that's because they want to make him a victim of their communist spite over some political attitude that he's adopted in the past. We're entering into a new era of extradition law, in which at the moment we stand very much on our own in the United Kingdom . . . There is no extradition treaty with the Soviet Union at this moment, and there never has been. I don't think there's ever been an extradition treaty with Russia,

not even in the Czar's days. And until the law is altered by Act
of Parliament, which is the only way to alter the law of Britain,
thus it will remain.

'The British public, and particularly those who were
children when it all happened,' continued Draper, 'or were not
even born, are not in the nature of things educated and
brought up in the history of what the Soviets suffered. The tale
of abomination that was committed by the agencies of the
Third Reich, in particular the SS and the security service and
the police regiments, and the local collaborators hired to do
their dirty work for them, passes the bounds of understanding,
as it almost passes the competence of the human race to relate
it in terms that do justice to the foulness of what they did.
Public opinion should be the ultimate factor in a democracy,
and we are a democracy. And if public opinion, without being
manipulated, misled, pressurised or bullied, arrives at the
conclusion that however long ago gross acts like genocide were
committed, if the perpetrator is safely living here as a British
citizen, it cannot really be overlooked for crimes so grievous.

'And if they are resident here, and the information is
produced to the Home Secretary and he pursues it, which he
should do, he is entitled by virtue of an Act of Parliament – the
British Nationality Act, 1981 – to deprive them of their acquired
British citizenship on the grounds that they have made false
particulars in a material point: not just some little detail about
age. For example, by stating when they applied for naturalisa-
tion that the applicant was a long-term victim of Nazi oppres-
sion, when in fact he was active in a special murder execution
squad operating under the Germans.'

Rabbi Marvin Hier agreed that men who found refuge in
Britain under the cover of genuine displaced refugees could
have their citizenship removed – 'They lied when they entered
Great Britain. If they are suspected war criminals, they didn't
state that when they entered the country, so they are not
entitled to any protection under the law.

'As for Antanas Gecas,' said Rabbi Hier in a sharp,

scathing New York accent, 'he is accused of mass murder. He lives in Edinburgh, where he admitted that his group, the 2nd Lithuanian Battalion, participated in the mass liquidation of Jews, only he claimed that he was always on the side on guard duty. Our information is that the whole unit did nothing for a living but kill civilians, and he was a platoon commander.

'If we can get tickets for speeding,' added the Rabbi, 'I think that mass murderers are entitled that governments should investigate their charges. It's preposterous for governments to say that legal technicalities . . . should the government of Great Britain, or any other government, say to us that they don't have an extradition treaty, and this is a difficult technicality – what do they have a parliament for? To overcome technicalities. The man has now been given citizenship in Britain, but he's been accused of mass murder, and we want to be able to furnish the legal technicalities to bring him to justice, or to deport him to a country that will.'

Home Secretary Douglas Hurd, captured on film at that news conference before Bob Tomlinson had stood and broken the cosy atmosphere with three rhetorical questions, defended his government in measured terms. 'We are very clear,' said the Conservative minister, 'that British courts don't have jurisdiction over crimes which are alleged to have been committed abroad by people who weren't, at the time of the alleged offence, UK citizens. I, of course, do not have jurisdiction in such cases.'

The question, 'Why not?' trailed his statement like a cloud, and remained unanswered. One of his predecessors, Merlyn Rees, attempted to correct Hurd's omission for Tomlinson and the Scottish film crew. 'In this respect,' he said, 'it is the Home Secretary that matters, and it is his job to open it up and take it further. Anyone who is not a British citizen would have to leave the country, they would have the right to a quasi-judicial appeal, but they would have to leave this country. And as I recall, they have the right to choose two countries who would receive them.'

The final, elegiac note was struck by Gerald Draper, his eyes moist and his lower lip trembling as he addressed the core of the issue in a voice which was invested with the sympathy of 40 years' immersion in the terrible deeds of the forgotten holocaust. 'If you but think,' he pleaded, 'of the talent. Of the geniuses, of the scientists, of the artists, of the writers, of the poets, and of the tens of scores of thousands of ordinary, decent human beings who perished in these genocide acts. One is moved to say, by God, what right does any man order that to be done to people? It is so ghastly that – ' his tone faltered, and he resurrected the sentence with a surge of bitter energy ' – I do not think that posterity can afford to forget it.'

This time they refused calls from interested outside agencies, and worked through the night to edit and prepare the film for transmission. They got translators into the office to confirm that what was said on camera complied with their Soviet translators' versions. Two of the Lithuanians thus summoned broke down in tears before the film.

Its broad structure devoted the first half of the programme to following Antanas Gecevicius's battalion from Lithuania to Byelorussia. As Gecas refused to be interviewed again, clips from that first and only chat before the cameras were used again, in brief. The rest of the evidence was left to the witnesses: to the women who had found their husbands' bodies; to the damning words of his former comrades-at-arms; to the Soviets who were trying to bring the Edinburgh pensioner to trial. After the commercial break the activities of Kyrylo Zvaritch were examined. It was then pointed out that while one man had died without facing his accusers, the other was still living.

And they called in the lawyer Len Murray from Scottish Television's media law advisors, Levy & McRae. His first response was: Antanas Gecas will be mad not to sue, immediately. 'This'll make wonderful litigation,' said Murray, 'because this is going to change the law of Great Britain.'

They all laughed, happily.

'It's phenomenal,' said a younger partner at Levy & McRae called Peter Watson, who Tomlinson had never seen before. 'It's a great piece of journalism. And legally, it's worth a fight.'

Watson would, in time, be called upon to justify his faith.

On 21 July, the day before the broadcast of *Crimes of War*, Bob Tomlinson flew with his family to a friend's villa in Portugal, to escape the nightmarish images which had accompanied his every waking moment – and some of his sleeping moments – for the better part of nine months. He was still upright, but at times he could not sleep with the bedroom light extinguished, and the fetid scents of Slutsk and dreams of the Ninth Fort at Kaunas followed him like smoke from Eastern Europe to London, Glasgow, home . . . Both he and his family needed a holiday.

So he found himself standing in swimming trunks, within hours of his holiday commencing, and hours away from the film going out, at a telephone in the office of an estate agent in a small Iberian village, fielding questions from the nervous representatives of the television watchdog body, the Independent Broadcasting Authority.

While other British tourists queued behind him for use of the telephone, and while office workers went about their business at the other side of the counter, Tomlinson was barking graphic details of war crimes into a Portuguese receiver . . . 'But I tell you, 8,000 people were slaughtered there, and he was in command . . . the bodies were piled high, you cannot cut that out . . . yes, they shot them in the nape of the neck . . . we know he was at Minsk, where hangings took place . . . yes, we can prove that people were burned alive. God, you should see what we didn't use . . .'

Behind him, the other visitors shuffled nervously in shorts, bikinis and white cotton suits on the cool, tiled floor. What was this Scotsman doing? Had the Costa del Crime come to this? 'Want to use this?' offered Tomlinson, holding out the phone.

'No, no . . . it's okay. You finish. Just go ahead . . .'

And so, 24 hours later, on 23 July, he was lying at a poolside in the midsummer sun when a courier arrived with a hand-transcribed telegram from the local post office. It was from Scottish Television's press office, and it told him that the programme had achieved a spectacular impact.

The press office did not exaggerate. PROBE WAR-CRIME NAZI IN BRITAIN, HURD TOLD, headlined the *Daily Mail*, continuing: 'Britain faced growing pressure last night to open up a major war-crimes investigation of a man branded "worse than Klaus Barbie".' TRIAL OF NAZI IN BRITAIN URGED echoed the *Independent*. 'Greville Janner, the Labour MP for Leicester East,' it read, 'said he was confident that the British public would support a trial of any alleged war criminals living here. "This country has not forgotten the war," he said. "It would not want to stand alone in not bringing war criminals to justice."'

RUSSIAN REQUEST FOR WAR CRIMINAL reported the *Observer*. Said the Scottish *Sunday Post*: CRIMES OF WAR – TV PROGRAMME MAY CHANGE LAW. The Bolton *Evening News* followed up its longstanding interest in its former reader, Kyrylo Zvaritch, with the headline: WAR CRIMES SENSATION!.

'After a glorious day of sunshine,' wrote TV reviewer Gordon Irving in the Scottish *Daily Record*, 'it was harrowing, in the hour before midnight, to view *Crimes of War*, made by Scottish Television. "Scenes are harrowing and distressing" we were warned. They were, indeed, thanks to diligent compilation and filming by a team from Glasgow . . .'

Rosemary Long in the Glasgow *Evening Times* said: 'So Antanas Gecevicius, alias Gecas, continues to live in Edinburgh, denying all participation in the murders of which he is accused. "The Russians are making it up for propaganda," he insists. Perhaps, but it was hard, watching the faces and listening to the voices of the witnesses, who seemed to breathe bleak despair and loss from every pore, not to feel that this was genuine testimony.' Just down the road in Antanas

Gecevicius's adopted home town, the television reviewer of the Edinburgh *Evening News* considered that Antanas Gecas 'must be wishing that television had never been invented'.

'*Crimes of War*,' wrote TV critic Nancy Banks-Smith in the *Guardian*, 'was a kick in the stomach . . . Scottish Television, who raised this spectre in a short programme earlier this year, has, with admirable teeth-in-the-trousers tenacity, followed up the story in Russia . . . In Slutsk, a place which sounds like waste being sluiced away, 8,000 were shot in a forest. An old woman, her face a clenched pink fist in a headscarf, remembered . . . The dead lay in trenches like charred sticks after a fire. A body was lifted from the earth flattened by 40 years. A big old woman in a red cardigan stood in a field and shouted, "He took children from their mothers, held them by the legs and shot them."' This was Piotrowski, who died in Bolton in 1984. 'There is something quite simple and serious that is offended by all this. The injustice is rank. It reeks to heaven.'

And that, thought Tomlinson, stretching out on the sunbed and yawning – contentedly unaware that even the English language daily newspaper serving the portion of British soil nearest to his Portuguese villa, the *Gibraltar Chronicle*, was headlining BRITAIN URGED TO ACT AGAINST NAZIS – and that, he thought, is that. Thank God it's over.

7

The makers of *Crimes of War* were alive to the fact that, having used documents and other printed material from within the deeply suspect world of the Soviet bureaucracy, they might be open to charges of gullibility, or worse: of the mortal journalistic sin of failing adequately to confirm their sources.

With this in mind, Bob Tomlinson had telephoned Rabbi Marvin Hier at the Simon Weisenthal Centre in Los Angeles before the documentary was broadcast.

'We have remarkable information about Gecas, and the 12th Lithuanian Battalion,' said the journalist.

Hier was interested. 'What will happen to it?'

'We'll edit it, submit it to Channel 4, have their producers go through it. Then we'll fix the transmission date. Rabbi . . . will you check the authenticity of some of the documents? Transcripts of trials in Lithuania – the Plunge trial, and others. Some of the evidence heard there is damning of Gecas. And some other material – I have it in the original, from the Soviets. Just a couple of pages of relatively unimportant material that I took away as samples, but I need them checking.'

'Send them to me.'

Hier had the documents examined by men with a deep interest in, and long familiarity with, official documents from the Union of Soviet Socialist Republics. He had them vetted by members of the Central Intelligence Agency. Then Hier called back to Scottish Television.

'They've dated the paper,' he said. 'It holds up, it's 20 years old. And the German documents they gave you: the paper is vintage 1941, and the ink has aged accordingly. They're good, they're sound. The CIA says so.'

The words came as a relief. A tint of paranoia coloured the closing weeks of prepapration for *Crimes of War*. Trickles of information leaked out of Scottish Television and into the press; hints and rumours about the war-crimes epic that the company was preparing to show. Many of the stories which appeared displayed a healthy scepticism; which was encouraged in a statement issued by Antanas Gecas through his lawyer, Nigel Duncan, on 24 July.

'Mr Gecas believes that his present troubles are the direct result of a campaign by Soviet agencies,' it read, adding portentously, 'taken altogether it does provide a foundation for slanders and vile innuendo for propaganda and sensationalist television programmes, but not conceivably as a foundation for any case at law in any court worthy of the name.' The statement went on to admit that Gecas had been present in Minsk in 1941, where he was a 'spectator' at some hangings, but denied that he had ever been in Slutsk.

'Throughout the war he was fighting for his country, Lithuania,' it said. He had no quarrel with the Jews. It was not the Jews who had invaded his country. It was not Jews who terrorised Lithuania and who deported his relatives and friends. He fought purely and solely for Lithuania.' Scottish Television had, said Gecas's solicitor, accepted material from Soviet sources 'in an astonishingly uncritical and unquestioning way'.

Tom Brown, a columnist in the *Daily Record*, the newspaper whose clipping had started it all for Tomlinson, commented on this statement:

It is unworthy to argue that the hunt for war criminals continues because it suits Israel's policies. Or that those who took part in the extermination of millions of Byelorussians, Lithuanians, Ukrainians and the rest are now victims of Soviet propaganda.

It is not just a matter for fellow Jews or Russians. We are all relatives of those who suffered in the holocaust. Just because those with responsibility have got away with it for 40 years, they cannot be allowed to get away with it for ever.

If a case is made against them, they must be brought face-to-face with their accusers – and our system must be changed to allow that to happen. If we do not condemn, we condone. And we would be as callous as the Nazi killers.

At Scottish Television, another line in Antanas Gecas's statement attracted attention. Their work was, allegedly, 'not [conceivable] as a foundation for any case at law'? Time would tell.

Bob and Margaret Tomlinson received an invitation shortly afterwards to travel to London and dine with Greville Janner, the MP and member of the All-Party War Crimes Group who had been so forthright before the Scottish Television cameras. There, in a West End restaurant, Tomlinson would meet for the first time the man who laid the trail for him: Neal Sher of the United States Office of Special Investigations; the man who had taken the vital statement from Antanas Gecas in Edinburgh in 1982. There, also, was former Home Secretary Merlyn Rees, and several other dignitaries from the All-Party War Crimes Group.

As the meal progressed Tomlinson mentioned that the CIA had seen and confirmed his Soviet documents. Immediately, Merlyn Rees passed him a note. It read, do not speak about anything secret in this room. It was just another restaurant, where MPs might meet, where members of the cabinet might hold informal gatherings . . . was it somebody else sitting at the table? Was it the waiter? Who on earth did this former holder of one of the four highest offices of state suspect? Tints of paranoia coloured the air, everywhere the issue of war crimes was raised: any news that broke too soon, the slightest piece of possible misinformation, could damage the whole case which was being built, brick by careful brick.

The caution was understandable. This small affair had rapidly become an international cause célèbre, and one which was therefore causing embarrassment to the British government. On 4 August, two weeks after the transmission of *Crimes of War*, the Prime Minister of Israel, Yitzhak Shamir, had announced that his government would be examining the case against Antanas Gecas with a view to seeking his extradition from Great Britain. Israel's Foreign Minister, Shimon Peres, had already assured the Weisenthal Centre: 'We will not let him [Gecas] go free. If the British will not prosecute then we will have to do it.'

Peres was backed up by Avraham Sharir, the Israeli justice minister, who announced that if Britain did nothing, the Israeli government would ensure that if Gecas was guilty, he would be punished. 'It is my duty,' said Sharir, 'as a Jew and as Minister of Justice to bring accused war criminals to trial.' Some British newspapers reported that the Israeli justice department was 'investigating a possible loophole in the Anglo-Israeli extradition arrangements' with an eye on arraigning Gecas in the Middle East. The British Home Office had acknowledged that it was examining the possibility that Antanas Gecas, in lying about his past, was liable to be stripped of citizenship – although, a Whitehall official added, this might have little practical effect as 'deportees have a choice of destination'.

Ephraim Zuroff had flown from the Simon Weisenthal Centre's offices in Israel in July and achieved a great deal of national publicity by going straight to Edinburgh, walking up Moston Terrace in the company of journalists and photographers, and knocking on Antanas Gecas's front door. While Gecas stayed hidden behind his venetian blinds, *The Times* reported, 'the door was opened only slightly and a woman told him that he should speak to their solicitor'. Antanas Gecas should be brought to justice, in Britain or elsewhere, Zuroff then announced. 'It is unthinkable that Britain should be a haven for Nazi war criminals.' His visit was the front-page lead in the *Jerusalem Post*.

The All-Party War Crimes Group had announced, just days earlier in London, that Klaus Barbie, the infamous 'Butcher of Lyons' whose trial in France attracted international attention, had been offered a job with British Intelligence after the war. A British major, who Barbie identified as 'Cooks', had approached Barbie through another former Nazi named Emil Hoffman and asked him to undertake intelligence work. Barbie had, he claimed, declined the offer. Rabbi Marvin Hier's response to those revelations was to insist that the crimes alleged against Antanas Gecas 'were worse than those for which Barbie had been given a life sentence'.

On 24 August the Soviet Foreign Ministry had formally lodged its application with the British government to have Gecas extradited to Lithuania to face trial there. Nataliya Kolesnikova had added that, if so required, witnesses in the Soviet Union could travel to Britain to be interviewed by UK authorities. Colonel Kolesnikova would, she insisted, also be prepared to visit Britain herself to help with inquiries into the Gecas case. A Home Office official described her offer as 'welcome and helpful'.

Tomlinson looked across the dinner table at Neal Sher, the representative of the United States government, and wondered yet again how Britain had manoeuvred itself into such an unusually grubby, insular corner. It was an uneasy gathering. Throughout their involvement in this intensely political affair, Scottish Television had tried to maintain a strictly impartial stance. From the moment of his first insistence to Guennadi Shabannikov that he was neither a communist nor a Jew (a line which he had found himself repeating time and again to officials throughout the USSR, not in his desire to denigrate such beliefs and backgrounds, but rather to stress his own independence of mind) Tomlinson had aspired to ride above the throng of motivated men and women who pushed the issue this way and that in accordance with their inherited grievances, or their dogma, or their cynicism, or their paymaster's will.

Professor Gerald Draper was also in the restaurant that evening, as proud and precise as ever, easing the night along for Tomlinson. Fascinated by Scottish Television's Soviet experience, he pursued question after question until the evening's end, when the Drapers and the Tomlinsons travelled back to the latter's Heathrow airport hotel in the highest of spirits. It was the last time that Tomlinson was to see Gerald Draper alive.

In the weeks before the release of *Crimes of War* Tomlinson had reached an uneasy truce with the civil servants of the Home Office. A steady barrage of telephone calls had failed to provoke the slightest comment from Whitehall, and finally a tacit deal was struck. We will lay off you, said Scottish Television, until after the film is broadcast. If, then, there is still no response, we will go hunting for those responsible. You will be getting a copy of the film, and of the script, said David Scott to the men in suits. Read it very carefully, he added, and ignore it at your peril.

Similarly, Antanas Gecas was approached, through his lawyers, for a further interview in the light of this new information. What is the new information? they wanted to know. Nervous of an interdict preventing the film from being broadcast, Scottish Television refused to reveal their findings in advance. We will release this information to you, came their response, only in the course of an interview with your client. No interview was granted.

There would be movement, lumbering and then hectic movement, both in Whitehall and in the offices of Antanas Gecas's legal representatives, in the fullness of time. It started with the usual leaks and rumours in the press, and with a small, slow court action which would prove to be of great importance. In October 1987, Antanas Gecas raised in the

Edinburgh Court of Session a defamation action against Times
Newspapers, claiming that two articles published in *The Times*
in August contained inaccuracies. He was reported at the time
to be looking for £50,000 damages. The action was then put on
the legal back-burner, where it would simmer for almost three
years, while the notional £50,000 inflated like Weimar currency
and interested lawyers tapped their pencils on their desks and
waited keenly.

In July 1987 the Simon Weisenthal Centre had handed
over to the Home Office a massive, 1,100-page dossier of
documents concerning war criminals and Great Britain.
Towards the end of November 1987 a series of peculiarly well-
co-ordinated stories appeared in national, London-based newspapers. 'Britain,' said one, 'looks set to shake off its "soft on
war criminals" label with the introduction of new laws to pave
the way for war-crimes trials similar to those seen recently in
France and Holland.

'Although, officially, the Home Office is saying this is
only one of three options under consideration to meet growing
demands for action against suspected Nazi criminals living in
Britain, it is understood to be the most favoured.

'The Home Secretary, Douglas Hurd, is expected to
announce the proposals before Christmas as an amendment to
the Criminal Justice Bill, currently on its way through
parliament.'

The *Observer* postulated on 22 November that 'war crimes
trials could be held in Britain within two years, as a result of
plans by Mr Douglas Hurd'. And on the following morning
the *Guardian* reported that the Home Secretary 'is believed to
favour an amendment to the Criminal Justice Bill allowing
prosecution of British citizens for crimes committed abroad,
even if they were foreign nationals at the time'. This would be,
the newspaper considered, 'a way of dealing with alleged Nazi
war criminals living in this country who have been exposed
during the past year . . . In August the Soviet Foreign Ministry
formally requested the extradition of Mr Antanas Gecas, a 71-

year-old Lithuanian who acquired British citizenship in the 1950s and lives in Edinburgh.'

As if to fan the fire, on 24 November the United Nations War Crimes Commission released for the first time its full list of 40,000 fugitive Nazi and Japanese war criminals. The list included the names of former UN Secretary-General and Austrian president Kurt Waldheim, and Antanas Gecas of Moston Terrace, Edinburgh.

The Christmas of 1987 came and went, and no announcement was made by the Home Office. In the early afternoon of 8 February 1988, Bob Tomlinson received a telephone call at Scottish Television from a member of the staff of the Home Secretary, Douglas Hurd – the same suave, patrician Conservative politician who had, just six months earlier, poured scorn on the notion of extraditing suspected war criminals, or of changing British law to accommodate trials at home, merely because of the 'allegations' of a television documentary.

'The Home Secretary will be making a statement in the House of Commons later today,' said the aide to Tomlinson. 'And he will be happy to give you the first opportunity to interview him about that statement.'

'What's it about?'

'It's about war crimes.'

'What's happening?'

'He's setting up a War Crimes Inquiry Team.'

Tomlinson breathed deeply. 'I'll take the interview.'

It was 2.30 p.m. The interview would have to be live, on a link between Glasgow and London. Tomlinson ran the length of the building punching the air like a footballer after a cup-final goal, grabbing people as he passed them, gabbling: 'Tell Ross Wilson to get in touch with me! I'll be with David Scott!'

He burst into Scott's office. 'We've done it! I think we've done it! Hurd's setting up an inquiry. He's offering a live interview tonight. I've said yes.'

Scott stood and looked out of the window. Then he turned, and there was a huge smile on his face. 'We've got them on the run,' he said. 'They're shaken. We haven't won this yet, but they're on the run.' He grinned at Tomlinson. 'Superb! Go and arrange the link.'

On the way into the newsroom Tomlinson met a delighted Wilson. 'We've won?' said the director, half in declaration, half in query.

'I think so. There's a long way to go, but . . . for the first time since 1948 a British government is doing something.'

Douglas Hurd duly announced to the House of Commons that afternoon that he was setting up a committee of inquiry which would be headed by Sir Thomas Hetherington, a former director of public prosecutions in England and Wales, and William Chalmers, a former crown agent in Scotland, the equivalent of England's DPP. They were two of the most senior law officers in the country, and they would investigate crimes committed by alleged war criminals living in Britain. Their remit was that they should then recommend to the British parliament whether or not the law of the United Kingdom should be changed in order that these people could be put on trial in the UK.

Extradition to the Soviet Union was still not possible, Douglas Hurd told the House of Commons. But . . . 'The courts in the United Kingdom at present do not have jurisdiction to try offences of murder and manslaughter committed abroad when the accused was not a British citizen at the time of the offence. If we were to prosecute in these cases we should need to extend the legislation of our courts.'

'The passage of time,' the Home Secretary went on, 'does not lessen the horror with which we now read about wartime atrocities, but it does inevitably complicate the investigation of any allegations which might be made.' Out of the 17 names of alleged war criminals which he had been given by the Simon Weisenthal Centre, the Home Secretary told parliament that it was thought that ten were still alive in the United Kingdom. He named no names.

Not every parliamentarian was delighted. The Conservative Ivor Stanbrook accused his Home Secretary of 'surrendering to a lobby whose main motives are hatred and revenge. This is a bad decision,' continued the right-wing MP, 'and one which is quite likely to lead to what others would call a witch hunt. British courts have never sought to try alleged crimes committed long ago by foreigners in a foreign land, for the very good reason that such evidence would be inadmissible in normal circumstances. Therefore it is very wrong for the government to make special arrangements for a special class of accused people who committed offences a long, long time ago which the British people would far rather not pursue.'

Stanbrook – whose argument, endlessly repeated in another chamber of the Houses of Parliament, would later create a minor constitutional crisis – was rebuked by his fellow Conservative Toby Jessel, who commented: 'Whatever else witches might or might not have done, they did not murder six million people.' Greville Janner welcomed the move 'to see that justice is done and evil monsters who may be among us are prosecuted'; and another Jewish MP, David Winnick, said that justice, not revenge, was the issue.

'In the light of its assessment,' concluded the Home Secretary, 'the inquiry team will advise whether the law should be amended in order to take jurisdiction over crimes allegedly committed overseas by persons now resident in this country.'

Douglas Hurd's qualifications and cautionary riders apart, it was stunning news. Tomlinson's delight was tempered by only one thing. The old man who had devoted much of his last 40 years to agitating for just such an inquiry, Professor Gerald Draper, had died. Between the showing of the film which turned out to be his final public word on the subject that had racked his very spine, and Douglas Hurd's announcement, he had passed away quietly in the south of England. *Crimes of War* and its results might yet serve as his epitaph.

Occasionally it seemed that the issue had achieved a dynamic of its own, that nothing and nobody could now slow it down. Skeletons were crawling out of cupboards across the

Western world. The evidence of an international committee of
six historians, commissioned by the United Nations to investigate the wartime activities of Austrian president and former
Nazi soldier Kurt Waldheim, was rocking governments even
as Douglas Hurd announced his inquiry. The historians implicated Waldheim in the torture and murder of six British
commandos in 1944. Grey-haired sisters of the dead appeared
on television and in the press. 'I have no doubt that Waldheim
knew what happened to my brother,' they would say bitterly.
'Ray was a hero. Waldheim is a beast.' Even the Conservative
press, occasionally reluctant to give credence to the allegations
of 'Jewish Nazi-hunters' and Soviet procurators, could not
ignore the brutal, cold-blooded destruction of half-a-dozen of
'our brave boys'.

And whenever a new allegation was heard, whenever the
matter of war crimes was forced once again into the limelight,
the name of Antanas Gecas arose. A week after the Home
Secretary's announcement, Ephraim Zuroff flew once again
from Jerusalem to Great Britain, this time to promote his book,
Occupation Nazi-hunter. Why, he was asked, did he devote his
life to persecuting old men?

'People should not think that the Jews are helpless,
defenceless, prime targets,' replied Zuroff. 'But it goes far
beyond that to a universal moral significance. They murdered
not only Jews but non-Jews as well. This goes to the heart of
what society is all about. No society which condones murder
can survive. As a society, what are you saying if you don't
prosecute war criminals? You are saying: "We'll let you live
out your life in tranquillity, and so be it." You are saying to a
prospective murderer growing up now: "Go ahead – you might
get away with it." If, on the other hand, you make serious
efforts 40 years later to bring murderers to justice, that's a
serious message to the population. Even an unsuccessful
prosecution is better than leaving them be. You've got to make
the point that governments will not countenance the murder
of innocent men, women and children. What are governments

established for? To protect the lives of citizens. If they can't do that they're worthless.'

Broaching the thorny problem of how many Nazi spear-carriers should be prosecuted along with their commanders, Zuroff said: 'Okay, not everyone's a Gecas. That doesn't mean they should be given a haven. Britain of all countries should know better. That's the ironic thing. Britain, which suffered so much during the war, has proved more reluctant [to prosecute] than other countries which have suffered far less. It's hard to understand.'

In September Antanas Gecas achieved an interim interdict which banned Ashford Press, Zuroff's publishers, from distributing *Occupation Nazi-hunter* in Scotland. Within weeks Zuroff was back in Scotland at the Edinburgh Court of Session, applying to have the ban lifted. If it was possible for such grave matters to find the level of farce, they did so on 12 October 1988.

As Zuroff stood in court listening to the case, the judge, Lord Cowie, suddenly developed a violent nose-bleed. He fled the Bench and the hearing was adjourned. At this point two messengers-at-arms walked up to Zuroff and tried to hand him a summons on behalf of Antanas Gecas, claiming £75,000 for defamation. Zuroff was quickly advised that he could not be served with a summons in court. He turned his back on the messengers, who were eagerly thrusting the paper upon him, and it fell on a seat. Then he walked out. 'To the best of my understanding,' the investigator told reporters outside, 'he cannot give it to me in a court of law. Why should I be part of something illegal?'

With a pleasing tip of their hats, Hetherington and Chalmers commenced their investigations at Scottish Television. They interviewed Wilson, Scott and Tomlinson. They took away copies of the film scripts. They queried the validity of witnesses. And then they went away to follow their own long trail towards the recommendations which would change the law of Britain.

But nothing more, in the short term, was heard from the lawyers of Antanas Gecas. It was slightly surprising. Why was the man remaining silent? He had been accused before a national television audience of mass murder, and had issued only a denial. Where was the outraged libel writ that Len Murray had dourly predicted and that Times Newspapers and Ephraim Zuroff had received before the ink was dry on their pages? The journalists had heard that, understandably, his wife and son were deeply upset, and Tomlinson felt this keenly.

And on those other rails, it became apparent that Hetherington and Chalmers were moving very quickly indeed. They had travelled to the Soviet Union and across the Atlantic. They were covering a great deal of important ground at breakneck speed. The two men's inquiries were finished in the early summer of 1989. They presented two reports that July: one to parliament, and the other one – which no amount of ferreting could uncover – which was Top Secret.

And they recommended to Prime Minister Margaret Thatcher and to the Houses of Commons and Lords that the law of Great Britain be changed in order that alleged war criminals could be put on trial within Britain, even for crimes that they had allegedly committed outside British territory. Without mentioning names, Sir Thomas Hetherington and William Chalmers said that they had examined seven cases in detail. One of their suspects had since died, but, their report insisted, there was sufficient evidence to proceed against three of the other six. More material should be gathered on the three remaining men, they added, and further inquiries should be made into no fewer than 75 other suspected war criminals at large in Great Britain.

Hetherington and Chalmers concluded of these unnamed men that their crimes 'are so monstrous that they cannot be

THE ANTANAS GECAS AFFAIR

condoned. To take no action would taint the UK with the slur of being a haven for war criminals.'

On 24 July 1989, Home Secretary Douglas Hurd announced to the House of Commons that two debates would be scheduled, giving Members of Parliament the opportunity to discuss and then to vote upon the principle of trying alleged war criminals on British soil. 'One can question,' Hurd told parliament, 'what will be achieved by prosecuting very old men so long after the events . . . my own belief, however, is that some crimes are so grave that our duty to bring criminals to justice cannot be set aside by passage of time.'

The announcement represented a comprehensive U-turn by the government of a lady who had notoriously pronounced herself to be 'not for turning'. It was welcomed by the Conservative MP Spencer Batiste, who prompted his fellows to vote in favour of a War Crimes Act. 'The important message,' said Batiste, 'that should come from this House is not one of revenge or of reopening old wounds, but the simple fact that those who have been guilty of horrendous crimes against humanity must never be able to feel that they are capable of achieving a safe haven in a civilised world.'

It was the first time in British history that such a recommendation had been made. Calls of congratulation came into Scottish Television from across the world. The Soviet Ambassador in London presented Tomlinson with a samovar as big as the FA Cup. The people of Jerusalem posted him a presentation book inscribed with the words: 'Blessed are the righteous, and there is none more righteous than yourself.' Bizarre, thought Tomlinson – a Scottish journalist sitting in Glasgow with a samovar from the Soviet Union in one hand and a bound volume from Israel in the other, while he opens an envelope containing an invitation from the Simon Weisenthal Centre to embark on a lecture tour of the United States of America. At least the superpowers seemed united on one point.

And still, over in Edinburgh, no further word or action

had arrived at Scottish Television from Moston Terrace.
Antanas Gecas had become, in a breathtakingly short period
of time, the most publicised and most wanted alleged war
criminal in the world who was still at liberty. And he was
apparently doing nothing. Perhaps he was right, they mused
at Scottish Television. If he made a bolt for it, if he made some
startling movement, then the police might be jolted into action.
Whatever his reasons, for the moment Antanas Gecas was
playing possum. While the media and the governments of
three continents reverberated with debate of the offences
which he and his fellows had been accused of committing,
while heads of state acted and laws were changed, while the
noose was surely tightening ever more securely around his
neck, the man at the centre of it all stayed quiet and alone in
the fastness of his Edinburgh suburb.

The silence ended with a bang on the night of Monday,
24 July 1989. To illustrate Douglas Hurd's announcement and
to issue a timely reminder of the issues which informed it,
Scottish Television altered their schedules to re-show *Crimes of
War* on that evening. Shortly before transmission at 10.35 p.m.
Scottish Television heard that Gecas's counsel, D. B. Robertson
QC, and junior counsel J. M. Simpson, were seeking an interim
interdict to have the programme banned. Like any large media
organisation Scottish Television – through their corporate solicitors Dundas & Wilson – had lodged caveats in the Court of
Session, which would normally stop any party turning up in
court seeking a banning order. The effect of such a caveat is
that when somebody applies for an interim interdict, the
person who has lodged the caveat will be informed when the
caveat is triggered. Nothing further was heard before the hour
of transmission, however, and so they went ahead with the
screening.

After 45 minutes, at 11.23, the screen went blank. An
announcer's voice told viewers that Scottish Television was
unable to continue with the documentary. 'An interim interdict

has been obtained in the Court of Session, Edinburgh, preventing us from doing so,' she said.

Just half an hour before the programme was due to go out a judge, Lord Prosser, had been dashed from his home to court, along with some officials, and the interim ban was allowed. The caveat had been triggered, but too late to prevent the first three-quarters of the film from going out. Simon Forrest, who was by then the Controller of Corporate Affairs for Scottish Television, told the press: 'It was transmitted because this was the film which sparked off the Home Office inquiry into various allegations. Later we were telephoned by our lawyer to say that the interedict was now in fact in place and from that point forward we could not transmit the programme. We immediately pulled the programme. We think that's the first time that a programme has actually been pulled off the air.'

In fact the programme would have been pulled shortly before 11.23 p.m., but the Scottish Television solicitor trying to telephone the station with the instructions to do so could not get through. The switchboard was jammed by other callers. A programme entitled *Prisoner, Cell Block H* had been pulled to make way for *Crimes of War*, and shortly after 11 o'clock a couple of dozen devout fans of that Australian soap opera were on the telephone, furiously demanding to know its whereabouts . . .

'We would like to finish showing what we started,' commented David Scott the following day. 'But we will have to look carefully at the terms of the interdict with our lawyers before a decision is made. Scottish Television was surprised by the steps taken by Mr Gecas's legal advisers shortly after ten o'clock on Monday night to stop the transmission of the programme. We had informed Mr Gecas's solicitor at 12.30 p.m. of our intention to broadcast the programme later that day.'

On Wednesday 26 June, Scottish Television had received through Dundas & Wilson a further communication from

Wilson, Terris & Co., acting on behalf of Antanas Gecas. A letter warned the TV station that legal action would be taken without warning unless an 'unequivocal assurance' was given that no further reference would be made to their client. Scottish Television refused to give any such assurance. Dundas & Wilson replied that they would attend to the terms of the current interdict against *Crimes of War*, 'but beyond that we can give no further undertaking'.

There was little doubt in anybody's mind as to what had sparked this sudden flurry of action. As if to stress the urgency of the question, in the same week that the interim interdict was gained and the second showing of *Crimes of War* was blacked out, William Chalmers spoke of his fears that 'delaying tactics' might lessen the chances of obtaining the convictions which his report had recommended. Nothing less was at stake than the international reputation of British justice, said Chalmers. 'In the inquiry we came to the conclusion that, having pride in our country and its reputation, we would be ashamed if a decision was taken that would mean Britain could truly be accused of being a haven for war criminals. If we want to hold our heads up high and say we are champions of justice we have to go ahead.'

A leading member of the Scottish Bar, Lionel Daiches QC, supported Chalmers's concerns. 'Time is of the essence,' said Daiches. 'In a year or two, because of the age of the witnesses, some of the available evidence must disappear.'

'We must move quickly,' Colonel Nataliya Kolesnikova had said, many years ago, 'people are growing old . . .' The words of a Soviet official were now being echoed by the highest legal voices in Great Britain.

The interdict against *Crimes of War* represented the first tentative shots in the legal hostilities between Scottish Television and Antanas Gecas. Battlelines began to be drawn. In August 1989 Scottish Television's legal representatives began to instruct a Queen's Counsel, Ranald Maclean, in their case, and legally speaking, the year was seen out with a low-level

defence of the interdict. Discussion proceeded about what
Scottish Television should do about it. David Scott wrote to his
old friend and colleague Len Murray of Scottish Television's
media lawyers Levy & McRae on 9 March 1990 that Scottish
Television would not attempt to have it recalled, on the
grounds that they were now highly unlikely to use the film
before any possible court case.

Murray's young colleague Peter Watson voiced the opinion that Gecas would not sue – 'He can't get legal aid for such
an action, and he's hardly wealthy.' It was a comment which
Watson, in the months to come, would wish that he had kept
to himself. There was also the possibility that the old Lithuanian might, merely through raising a defamation action,
prevent a criminal case being brought against him – whether
he won or lost the civil case. One set of evidence would be
much the same as the other; an earlier civil case would
therefore prejudice a later criminal action. It could be argued
that, if he was found 'guilty' in a defamation action, he could
not get a fair trial in a later criminal case. And if his lawyers in
the former were acting on a speculative basis, what did he
stand to lose?

But Antanas Gecas, it began to appear, might have been better
advised to let his natural span ebb peacefully away while the
world waited for Westminster to make up its mind. For the
twin chambers of the Houses of Commons and Lords were, it
soon became obvious, pulling in different directions.

Both bodies debated the issue in the first two weeks of
December 1989, and they reached dramatically different conclusions. The elected House of Commons, with MPs granted a
free vote by their party whips, conducted a passionate discussion. Most of the government supported the Hetherington/
Chalmers report. Douglas Hurd had moved on in a cabinet
reshuffle to become Foreign Secretary, but his replacement at
the Home Office, David Waddington, supported the Damas-
cene Hurd line. 'Sometimes one is brought face to face with

facts that cannot be buried,' Home Secretary Waddington told the Commons. 'And I do not believe that the Hetherington report can just be interred. I cannot believe that we should now fail to give jurisdiction to our courts so that, if the independent prosecution authorities so decide, the issue of guilt or innocence can be properly determined.' The *Daily Telegraph* would later note that '[Mr Waddington's] view is understood to have been influenced, at least in part, by evidence contained in the confidential part of the Hetherington/Chalmers report, which set out the cases against a handful of individuals'.

David Waddington was supported on the government benches by Prime Minister Margaret Thatcher and all but three of her cabinet. Of those three who opposed the principle of a War Crimes Bill, it would be of some interest to students of later inactivity to note that they included the then Chancellor of the Exchequer and future Prime Minister, John Major.

The leader of the Labour opposition, Neil Kinnock, supported the principle of a Bill, as did his deputy, Roy Hattersley; while the liberal middle ground, spearheaded by Paddy Ashdown, Dr David Owen, and the Conservative former Prime Minister Edward Heath, opposed the notion. The main figures had already been dealt with at Nuremburg, argued Mr Heath, adding darkly: 'There has been enormous pressure on this, and it has all come from California. We know all about that.'

When the Commons vote came it was surprisingly decisive: 348 MPs voted in favour of the principle of enabling war-crimes trials to take place in Great Britain; only 123 against. 'It was a startling majority,' commented the Father of the House, the Conservative Sir Bernard Braine. 'We are very pleased. The Hetherington report said we should get moving quickly. Now we must. The majority of people in this country have no idea of the awfulness of what was done.'

But Sir Bernard Braine, like many of his colleagues, had reckoned without the dark prejudices which were being aired in the second, unelected legislative chamber: the House of

Lords. This was not to be a happy or a creditable episode in the history of that strange body. Its powers were, as ever, limited to delay and attempted amendment; but the debates on war crimes which stretched the patience of the House of Commons beyond breaking point did nothing to suggest that the Lords were worthy even of those small residual weapons.

For day after day in the House of Lords, septuagenarians and octogenarians stood to chorus that they could not see how men of their own age and younger were fit to take the stand in a war-crimes trial and give reliable testimony. A strong dose of anti-semitism was also introduced to the considerations of the second chamber. 'Some of the victims,' offered Lady Saltoun of Abernethy, 'Christian or otherwise, might have preferred to forget [the holocaust]. But Weisenthal did not take that into account when he appointed himself as their vindicator. Is it decent and proper,' wondered Lady Saltoun, 'that we should take such a step in order to enable aliens to be revenged on other aliens for something done in a foreign country nearly half a century ago?'

Lord Hankey echoed Lady Saltoun's concern about the unreasonableness of alien vengeance. 'I understand only too well,' he assured his fellow peers, 'the eye for an eye and tooth for a tooth philosophy behind such prosecutions.' Nobody stood to remind Lord Hankey that, far from demanding an eye for an eye, the Hetherington/Chalmers report had merely recommended prosecutions for crimes of mass murder, in a country where the death penalty had not existed since 1965, and he cheerfully continued: 'The same idea arises instinctively in one's breast when one thinks about what one has seen, but for good or ill I recoil from it. I do not think that our countrymen enjoy that approach. It is entirely against our good Christian upbringing and philosophy.'

After the good and English Christian Lord Hankey, what availed it to protest the Chief Rabbi, Lord Jacobovits, that: 'My faith abhors vengeance. The Law of Moses denounces as a grave moral offence the bearing of a grudge or the taking of revenge.'

Other peers, recalling their own experiences in the government and civil service of the 1940s, understandably sought to justify their own failure to act 40 years earlier. 'When that huge movement was occurring,' explained Lord Wilberforce, a former administrator in occupied Germany and Austria, of the post-war refugee problem, 'it was perfectly plain to everyone that among these people there may be some who had participated to some degree in war crimes.' They had not been acted against, said Lord Wilberforce, because it would have been 'impractical'.

Lord Houghton thought that war criminals would not receive a fair trial, and puzzlingly characterised Lord Jacobovits's contribution as 'dreadful in its literal sense. It was the voice of the Old Testament as I was taught it, and Jehovah was not a kindly god . . . I thought that the noble Lord Chief Rabbi made the kind of speech that one could expect to hear from the steps of the guillotine or the scaffold, except that he did not call for mercy upon their souls . . .'

After a day or two of such elevated debate, it came as no great surprise when the House of Lords rejected the principle of trying war criminals. The War Crimes Bill was nonetheless formulated and put before the House of Commons for a first reading in March 1990. It was approved by another huge majority of 273 votes to 60. It was then forwarded to the House of Lords on 4 June 1990. The peers rejected it, by an unashamed majority of 133.

People began to talk of a constitutional crisis. It was a curious circumstance: a Conservative government, traditionally supportive of and fully supported by the House of Lords, being baulked at every turn in its efforts to pass into law a Bill which had the support of the Prime Minister, the Home Secretary, and the great majority of the House of Commons.

Margaret Thatcher and Home Secretary David Waddington took unprecedented action. They agreed to return the War Crimes Bill to the House of Lords for a second time. If the peers proved unrepentant after this, their third debate on the subject, they would dust down and invoke the Parliament Act. This little-known measure was first introduced by the Liberal Prime Minister Lloyd George in 1911, as a last means of passing his budget through Parliament. It simply allowed the Commons to overrule the Lords after a second negation by the latter. The Parliament Act had last been brought out of its cupboard in 1949, when a Labour government amended it. It had never been invoked by a Conservative government.

On 1 May 1991 the House of Lords was given its final chance to bow to the inevitable: to vote for the War Crimes Bill, or to see itself humiliated and its very role brought into question by the invocation of the Parliament Act by a Conservative Prime Minister. Unbowed, the House of Lords defeated the War Crimes Bill for a second time, by a reduced majority of 131 to 109 – the low figures reflecting the nervousness of many peers at stirring up a constitutional imbroglio. But it was done, and the House of Commons duly retaliated.

On the afternoon of the same day the Speaker of the House of Commons, Mr Bernard Weatherill, told MPs: 'The House of Lords will be asked to return the Bill to us, where it will be prepared for royal assent. No further proceedings are required in the Commons.' There was a short flurry of uproar from both sides of the debate. Ivor Stanbrook complained that the Parliament Act was 'really intended for issues of great constitutional importance and not for the very narrow and rather unworthy purpose of facilitating the prosecution of a few old men for crimes committed 50 years ago thousands of miles away'. The third Home Secretary to juggle with this aging but still contentious measure, Kenneth Baker, insisted that 'many people feel very strongly indeed that when people have committed crimes against humanity involving thousands of people and the alleged criminals are living in this country, they should be brought to justice'.

The Conservative Robert Adley mourned that: 'Many of us are thoroughly ashamed to be sitting on these benches and finding a Conservative government doing what it's doing.' Labour's Dennis Skinner wanted to know: 'What's the point of having a General Election for 650 MPs when the people down the road, 1,100 of them, in there for life and not one of them elected by anybody outside this place, are telling the elected House of Commons what to do? Let's get rid of them.' And Greville Janner urged the authorities to 'move with all possible speed and diligence. Too much time has passed for there to be any further delay.'

And that, after a minor parliamentary earthquake, was that. NAZI SUSPECTS FACE TRIALS AS LORDS SNUBBED read the headlines on 2 May 1991. 'The first arrests could be made within months, followed by Nuremburg-style trials at the Old Bailey,' postulated the stories.

That dull October morning in 1986 which had found Bob Tomlinson incredulously scanning a short report in the *Daily Record* had resulted in the creation of a piece of British constitutional history. And in the changing of British law. From that day onwards Antanas Gecas and his ilk were liable to be prosecuted. Britain was no longer a Nazi safehouse.

The moving camera films, and having filmed, moves on . . . all of the men and women who had commissioned, researched, filmed, presented, directed and publicised Scottish Television's two documentaries on war criminals found themselves, in the natural, professional course of events, soon doing other things.

Tomlinson was making a series of social-campaigning documentaries, far removed from the traumas of Slutsk and the Kaunas forts, while the War Crimes Bill limped tortuously through its Westminster proceedings. He watched with interest, but without personal involvement. He had asked David Scott if he could be taken off the case, and the producer agreed. The Nazi-hunter tag, never welcome, had become an unrequested burden; and the story itself had been dangerously close to consuming all of his working life and the better part of his leisure.

He was hauled back into the case as the result of an unpredicted – and as it turned out, portentous – legal action. In its coverage of the affair, *The Times* had carelessly reported back in 1987 that Antanas Gecas had been a member of the Ukrainian SS, and that he wore an SS tattoo. The Lithuanian's legal representatives sprang, and the law took its weary course. In May 1990 Tomlinson was called as a witness to the trial, which was scheduled for early June. A former colleague, Charles Wilson, was editing *The Times*. He telephoned.

'I think you've got it wrong,' said Tomlinson. 'The guy is a mass murderer. The rest of it, the Ukrainian SS, the tattoo and that, it's irrelevant – but it's wrong.'

For the first time he began to realise the essence of defamation action. It was as much about fine detail as basic truths. *The Times* could not be faulted in its overall assessment of Gecas's past, but the newspaper could be hung out to dry by somebody who they had correctly identified as a war criminal, as the result of two small, incidental errors. Tomlinson felt sorry for Tom Bower, *The Times* reporter. And simultaneously, he felt unnerved.

He was the first witness called. *Crimes of War* was to be shown by the defence to the Court of Session, and that disturbed Tomlinson. It felt as if Scottish Television were being set up to carry the can for *The Times*. David Scott called the newspaper's solicitors to gain assurances that Tomlinson would be protected in court. Scottish Television were not on trial.

The problem never arose. On 5 June 1990 – the day after the House of Lords first rejected the War Crimes Bill – Bob Tomlinson arrived at the Court of Session in Edinburgh to be told that *The Times* were about to settle the defamation – which, from modest acorns, had grown into an action which was widely reported as demanding £600,000 – out of court. They apologised in court before the case started, for saying that

Gecas had been in the Ukrainian SS and that he had an identifying SS tattoo. Brian Gill QC, counsel for *The Times*, said: 'The defenders now acknowledge that in respect of these specific matters, the articles were inaccurate. The defenders retract and apologise for these specific inaccuracies.' Times Newspapers' lawyers announced that the deal involved no money being paid to Gecas other than a contribution towards his legal costs.

Coming when it did, just 24 hours after the Lords rejected the Commons' attempt to put a War Crimes Act on the statute book, this apology marked a promising couple of days for Antanas Gecas. So far as Tomlinson was concerned, it also set a worrying precedent. Alastair Brett, Times Newspapers' company solicitor, explained that their decision not to fight was prompted by the fact that 'Mr Gecas's lawyers have been working on a speculative basis – if they did not win the case they did not get paid – but *The Times* has to take a commercial view of the situation. The settlement has to be regarded as satisfactory in a Scottish legal system which allows fees to be charged on a no-win, no-fee basis. That makes life extremely difficult when the onus is on the publishers, whose defence was that what was written was true. Evidence would have to be brought in from Lithuania and Germany and *The Times* would have run up a substantial bill – perhaps as much as £500,000 – with the likelihood of recovering nothing from Mr Gecas.' That may have been the first time that Bob Tomlinson took notice of the principle of cost-consciousness in defending libel actions. It would not be the last.

Tomlinson found himself sitting in court behind Gecas's counsel. He leaned forward.

'What about the mass murders?' he whispered.

'You can see what's happening,' replied the counsel. 'You get it? I hope your colleagues on the press benches understand this as well.'

OLD SOLDIER WINS LIBEL CASE, read the headline in one national newspaper on the following morning. Few of the papers seemed willing to grasp the fact that *The Times* was not apologising for naming Gecas as a mass murderer, but rather for two comparatively trivial points of identification.

That small climbdown in the Court of Session proved a turning point. Five weeks later Antanas Gecas and his legal representatives finally girded up their loins and turned towards the television company which, if truth be told, had been their main concern since 1986. All of the earlier skirmishes, the writs served on Ephraim Zuroff and on *The Times*, the blacking out of broadcasts and the muttered threats, had been leading to just one thing: a necessary, decisive assault on Scottish Television. Almost unwittingly, the company at Cowcaddens had become the flagship of the British war-crimes reform fleet. Sink it, and the rest would surely flee.

8

On holiday in the July of 1990, Bob Tomlinson telephoned his mother. They talked inconsequentially for several minutes, then . . .

'Oh,' she said, 'there's something in the papers. Gecas is suing you for six hundred thousand pounds.'

Scottish Television had received the letter from Wilson, Terris & Co. on 11 July 1990. It had been sent by recorded delivery. It read:

We are instructed by Anthony Gecas to write in relation to a programme titled *Crimes of War* made by you and screened on 23 and 25 July 1987, and again on 24 July 1989.

This programme made personal reference to our client as having personally participated in the unlawful and unwarranted mass killings in cold blood of innocent civilians in Lithuania and Byelorussia while serving with the Lithuanian Police Battalion. This programme also implied that Mr Gecas was a Nazi and that he supported and was a participant in the killing of innocent civilians of the Jewish faith.

These allegations screened by you are untrue. They amount to a very serious defamation of our client. We have to request that you submit your proposals for an apology. Further having regard to the gravity of the allegations made against a man who, having fought beside the Germans in order to drive the Russians from his country of Lithuania and their illegal occupation thereof, surrendered to the Allies in Italy where he

was commissioned in the Polish forces and then fought in Italy
for the Allied cause . . .

The wide publicity involved in screening this programme
thrice, and the serious effect this has had on his feelings and
reputation, our client is entitled to compensation as well as an
apology. In addition therefore to an apology we must ask you
to submit your proposal for an amount of damages. Failing a
satisfactory reply within four days, our instructions are to raise
defamation proceedings without further warning.

That letter had been passed on, as ever, to Levy & McRae
in Glasgow, the day-to-day media legal advisers to Scottish
Television. The function of this firm was routinely to check the
legality of – and make suitable recommendations for – programmes such as documentaries, news features, and current
affairs.

Scottish Television also had a firm of corporate solicitors,
the large and prestigious Edinburgh company of Dundas &
Wilson. The Gecas case would bring the two law firms
together, effectively for the first time. Levy & McRae had a
particular interest in this case, as it had been their original
advice to approve the broadcast of *Crimes of War*, and could
perform in the litigation arena as effectively as the Edinburgh
firm. It would be no small motivation in this particular case for
them to recall occasionally that their firm had been founded by
one Abraham Levy, and that it still enjoyed the custom of
many Jewish clients, some of whom were survivors of the
holocaust.

Len Murray at Levy & McRae had been the apprentice
master of Peter Watson, training him, the younger man freely
acknowledged, 'in every aspect of the law', particularly the
arts of representing and advising clients in the silver world of
media law, which he had introduced to the firm – and in which
area the company had thrived, coming to represent not only
Scottish Television but also Border Television, Channel 4, and
various newspaper stables. These two lawyers would between

them prepare much of Scottish Television's case. They were aware that this particular litigation would draw each of them, and their firm, into new and untested grounds – how new, how untested, and precisely how important was yet to be seen, when that summons arrived from Wilson, Terris & Co. in July 1990.

Murray had stepped back from full-time work with the company by 1990, and was now a consultant contributing chiefly as an advisor. Peter Watson, who would find himself steering Scottish Television's case through court in Murray's absence, was 36 years old in 1990, and had grown fascinated by media law under the tutelage of Murray, to whose friend-ship and advice the younger man would always bow. Slowly, he had become exposed to the more challenging aspects of the work involved, which had by 1990 twice seen the firm at the House of Lords. He felt that his talents were complementary to those of Murray, his own being a fine eye for detail and technicalities, Murray's being intuitive in judgement and assessment. By 1990, Peter Watson felt himself ready for some 'high-octane' legal practice. He was about to get it.

When the Antanas Gecas case came along Levy and McRae were elevating both their ambitions and their facilities. They had determined to seek out more specialist, high-quality, high-paid work. Their offices were being newly computerised, their information technology improved, their law library expanded. Aware of accusations that they were newly arrived yuppies on the scene, they were anxious to confirm their reputation in media law. Those ambitions, corporate and personal, would shortly be put to the test.

On 13 July the *Scotsman*, which seemed often to carry clear accounts of the movements and intentions of Antanas Gecas, reported that he was looking for a million pounds from Scottish Television. On 23 July 1990 Peter Watson wrote from Levy & McRae in Glasgow to Dundas & Wilson reporting that Scottish Television had been served with a summons in the instance of 'Antony Gecas', and asking them to accept instructions 'to act as our Edinburgh agents on behalf of Scottish Television'. The interim interdict had been what the lawyers suspected all along: the precursor to the major battle which was now about to commence. Scotland's biggest-ever defamation action, and the most publicised and discussed civil case of the century, was put underway in July 1990.

Watson began his campaign by discussing their case with the representatives of *The Times*. It quickly became clear that the newspaper had been in possession of very little hard information with which to mount a valid defence. They had not succeeded in getting a commission to take evidence abroad, and were therefore largely dependent upon 'secondary' evidence. These were important lessons. Derek Currie of *The Times* legal team opened up his files to Watson, and put the young lawyer in touch with every helpful contact in his book, saving Levy & McRae great amounts of time and effort.

It seemed almost unreal to Tomlinson, as if the threat of a libel suit for £600,000, or a million pounds – or any sum you cared to pluck from the air – was something chimerical – or, if it was really there, something which would pass like a bad dream. He continued with his other, ordinary work. In August 1990 he was woken up to reality. Scottish Television received a stern letter from Peter Watson which insisted that it was most important that the television company got on the road and collected witness statements. Why such a panic? thought Tomlinson. Typical lawyers, trying to put the frighteners on you . . .

A meeting was called at Scottish Television on 7 August. Scottish Television was shortly to be renewing its franchise to broadcast commercial television to the majority of the population of Scotland, and for this reason among others it was argued that it would be better to take 'a long view' of the action. To be seen to climb down from such a crucial moral high ground could affect even the base commercial life of the station. The long view was adopted. It seemed a clear, easy course, stretching ahead: legal routines and niceties to be observed, witnesses to be gathered, tactics to be determined. Nobody at that meeting could guess what difficulties lay before them, what obstacles as unforeseen as the collapse of the second most powerful state in the world, would be placed in their path.

Scott and Tomlinson sat there, the former as ever like the headmaster newly arrived in a turbulent classroom – Peter Watson could seldom forget, in Scott's presence, that one of the first things the big producer had ever said to him was that as a media lawyer his job was not to hone the news into mediocrity, but to get the news out. So far as Scott was concerned, if his company had transmitted a documentary programme, then axiomatically it was well researched. And if it was well researched, it would withstand the test of litigation. This court case would, he insisted to the final judgement, be fought and won.

Tomlinson frankly allowed most of what was said to pass over his head. He believed implicitly in the strength and accuracy of his story. He could see no way in which Antanas Gecas would mount a convincing attack upon his work. He believed that *The Times* had let the side down by settling out of court, and that if Scottish Television held their ground then surely this whole disturbance would just . . . go away. Word had arrived at Scottish Television that Antanas Gecas's home was owned by his wife, that he had no assets, no finances with which to fight. So what's the problem? thought Bob Tomlinson. He's guilty, and he can't afford to sue us. What the hell . . .

Peter Watson looked across at the investigative journalist. It would be rather more than a slap in the face if this goes against him, he thought. It would be a cause of unbearable shame, to be stigmatised as having got it all wrong. All the awards and the previous praise could just as well be flushed away. Watson was coming to like Scott and Tomlinson. The first, from an initial response of something close to fear, he had come to recognise as a powerful professional who stood not beside, but in front of his colleagues when the flak flew.

And Tomlinson was an irresistibly sympathetic character – easy going, generous and honest. He could well have done without this litigation, at his time of life, at this point in his career, mused the 36-year-old lawyer.

'His legal team might be on a no-win, no-fee agreement,' said somebody in the room.

Tomlinson sat up. He remembered the words of *The Times* solicitor when he conceded their case to Antanas Gecas on the grounds that it would cost more to fight than to surrender. 'That means they'll come after us with nothing to lose?'

'Correct.'

Tomlinson felt the first cold fingers of doubt.

Two weeks later they met with counsel again. Peter Watson was becoming increasingly insistent that Tomlinson should return to the Soviet Union with a translator and a solicitor to garner statements and supportive evidence. Tomlinson still did not fully share the young lawyer's agitation. If Tomlinson was becoming agitated about anything, it was with the nervous insistence of Peter Watson.

By the end of that second meeting, which was held at Scottish Television, Tomlinson understood. Talk of money had entered the argument. There had been occasional mention of the possibility of Scottish Television winning only a Pyrrhic victory over Antanas Gecas, if it spent far more on defending itself than it could ever recover. This Pyrrhic victory notion was rejected by Tomlinson, and by Peter Watson. 'It would be more than that,' the latter insisted, 'if it defends the reputation of the company as a programme-maker. There is also the important factor of a small company being prepared to stand by a programme exposing a war criminal. In Scotland we have Jewish families.' Jewish families, the lawyer would later learn, who had lost relatives to none other than Antanas Gecas's 12th Lithuanian Battalion. Watson increasingly came to regard the case as being one not just of professional, but of personal and moral importance.

But the subject of money still arose.

It was suggested by a member of the legal team that, since it would cost Scottish Television a great deal of money just to prove that they had got it right, and since there was no chance of that money being recovered, it might well be that they should pay Gecas nuisance money.

Tomlinson stood up. 'For a start,' he said hotly, 'there ought to be television cameras here, recording this; because this is one of the first legal meetings to take place regarding what will effectively be the first war-crimes trial to take place in Britain.'

The others looked at him as at a maniac. He's still looking for a story, their expressions said.

'I'm serious about this,' continued Tomlinson. 'I really do think we should have a camera running here.' The expressions around the table did not alter. 'And what is this nuisance money?' he went on. 'Are you suggesting we should pay Gecas money because he's a nuisance to us?'

The lawyer's reply was that they should consider paying Gecas because they had been a nuisance to him, rather than lose the money in fighting a very costly litigation.

After the meeting Tomlinson and one of the lawyers walked together along a corridor towards Scottish Television's reception desks. When Tomlinson asked again why they should settle out of court, he was told that Scottish Television's insurers faced a choice between funding an extremely costly case, costing up to half a million pounds, and paying Gecas £50,000 or £100,000. To Tomlinson's dismay, there could be no guarantee that a settlement wouldn't be made; it was a matter for Scottish Television and their insurers.

Tomlinson's understanding of the nature of this libel business, an understanding which had begun with *The Times* affair in June and had been nurtured by the first meeting at the offices of Levy & McRae, might never be complete, but he was beginning to grasp the basics. The action raised by Antanas Gecas was not and never had been concerned with the questions: was he a mass murderer? was he involved in the slaughter at Slutsk? did he help to hang teenagers and women at Minsk?

Those questions were apparently, in the world of the law, almost irrelevant. His instinct was to cry out, where the hell is the justice in this? All of the evidence was stacked against Antanas Gecas, but because it might be cheaper for Scottish Television and their insurers to pay him off rather than to fight the case, that evidence might never be brought into court. There would be no vindication of the story – worse, the public would be left with the overriding impression that Antanas Gecas had been wronged, that Scottish Television had lied. OLD SOLDIER WINS LIBEL CASE . . . and the old soldier from the murder squad that had been the 12th Lithuanian Auxiliary Battalion would walk away with £50,000–£100,000 of Scottish Television's money, as the result of Tomlinson's work, Wilson's work, Scott's work, as the result of a film crew slogging through the killing fields of the occupied Soviet Union.

Where is the justice in this? Tomlinson's sleepless nights returned. He knew how it would appear in the press; and every time in the past that he had read '. . . the Daily Bugle settled out of court yesterday with . . .', he had assumed – with most of the rest of the world – that the Daily Bugle and its cackhanded reporters had got it wrong, made it up, failed to check sources, been taken for a ride. So now he knew that it did not always mean that. So what? Try telling the readers.

Not until December 1991 would his qualms be finally laid to rest. In that month, after almost a full year of research and gathering evidence, Tomlinson, Scott and the solicitor Len Murray met in the Court of Session with their newly appointed Queen's Counsel, Colin Campbell, and his junior, Richard Keen, who had replaced Gerry Moynihan and Brian Gill two months earlier. The message from the lawyers was sobering. They were told that, at this stage, they did not have a case. All their documents and interviews on camera were quite inadmissible as evidence. Their witnesses would have to repeat everything they had said in a courtroom; in a Scottish courtroom.

Two weeks later another meeting was arranged with Campbell, and with the insurers. David Scott arranged to see the insurers beforehand, without the Queen's Counsel being present. When the three insurance men arrived, Scott told them that, whatever the views of the lawyers, Scottish Television would win its case. He outlined the evidence available to Scottish Television. The insurers looked convinced as the party continued on to the Court of Session to meet Campbell and Keen. They were taken by their counsel down to rooms in the basement, past groups of advocates and their clients.

The message from the lawyers was similar to two weeks earlier. Before they would consider taking the case, they would require a full-time team of solicitors working with a full-time team from Scottish Television – which would include Bob Tomlinson. Even if they won, it was going to cost a fortune.

The three men left the room like a jury, to consider their verdict in privacy. If those three men come back in here and say, we are going to pay Gecas off, thought Tomlinson, the story will be entirely discredited. He will be off the hook. My career will be stuffed. Scottish Television will be wiping egg from its face.

When they returned, Colin Campbell asked them if they had reached a decision.

'Yes.' One of the insurers spoke quickly. 'We have decided to go with it.'

Acting in a manner that David Scott later chided as 'extremely uncool', Tomlinson smashed his fist on the table and shouted: 'Yes!'

'Excuse Bob,' said Scott, laughing. 'He's pleased.'

He was. There would be no running away, no cheap settlement. The issue could be decided in a court of law, and whatever the finicky vagaries of the law, it would at least offer the opportunity to prove a case against an alleged war criminal. At least and, in the case of Great Britain, at last. A court case . . . the War Crimes Group had dreamed of such an event. The Simon Weisenthal Centre's representatives had discussed it as they might talk of an unlikely gift from God.

The insurance men were asked if they wanted to stay and listen to the briefing.

'No, no, you carry on. We're happy with what's happening.' And, their decision taken, they left the basement room in the Court of Session. Much later, Tomlinson would meet one of those three wise men again.

'Why did you take that decision?' he asked. 'Surely it would have been much easier for you just to give him £100,000 and tell him to go away.'

'Well,' said the man, 'people have prejudices about insurance companies – just as they do about journalists. They think we'll always take the easy, cheap way out, regardless of principle. We just happened to believe that you had got it right, and we wanted to send a signal to everyone that when a story like yours does happen to be true, plaintiffs cannot come sniffing around hoping for a quick buck. That was it, really. You had a case and he did not, and we wanted to put an end to people bringing actions just in the hope of being paid off.'

'You'd better get your passport and visa stamps ready,' said David Scott to Tomlinson as they crossed the road outside the Court of Session. 'It sounds like you're going to be a busy man.' On the following day Scott found a private room for Tomlinson at Scottish Television, to which only the two men would have access. Its number was XG 16. The filing cabinets were double locked. Two keys were issued, and a master-key left with a member of the security staff. In XG 16, the campaign to win the most important libel action ever faced by Scottish Television was based.

But those last moments of detail, that final pruning of the defence was 12 months away and unforeseen in the December of 1990. At that point there was, to the journalist, simply a straight job of work to be done, uncluttered by insurers and Queen's Counsel and nagging solicitors. Tomlinson had telephoned the Lithuanian translator, a Glasgow-born man named Alan Henderson. He agreed to work with the Scottish Television legal team. Simultaneously, over at the Crown Office in

Edinburgh, the War Crimes Police Unit, armed with the Hetherington Report's secret submission – and, incidentally, also occasionally employing the services of interpreter Henderson – was involved in its own investigations.

On 2 November 1990 Tomlinson, Gerry Moynihan and John Innes of Dundas & Wilson, Peter Watson and David Scott met in Levy & McRae's offices high above the centre of Glasgow to discuss Tomlinson's return to the Soviet Union in January. They discussed the possibility that the War Crimes Bill would be mentioned in the forthcoming Queen's Speech at the opening of Parliament. They agreed that no such Bill would be likely to be put forward before June 1991. It was clear that Antanas Gecas was one of the three people actively being considered for prosecution should the state take such a step.

On one thing they were all agreed. Secondary evidence, such as depositions and written statements, would be useful. But depositions and written statements alone would never win this case; particularly if they were tainted by the hand of the Soviet KGB. Live witnesses were essential. Those talking heads that the documentary programmes had tried assiduously to avoid, for fear of boring an audience, were the meat and drink of a courtroom hearing. Live witnesses alone could win or lose the case. No matter how much trawling it required of the Eastern European plains, they must be produced, either in Scotland or – without precedent – before a Scottish court hearing in the Soviet Union. They would have to travel the world to find their witnesses; to collect their statements; and to bring them, if possible, to Edinburgh. They were in search not just of a diaspora of Jewish survivors scattered from Israel to the United States, but another, more sinister diaspora of their former persecutors, hidden from retribution. And it was finally decided to send the experienced Len Murray to the Soviet Union with Tomlinson and Henderson. Visas were obtained for the three men and an itinerary arranged. The road ahead still seemed clear. Not easy, but not yet obstructed.

9

On 5 January 1991 Len Murray, Bob Tomlinson, and Alan Henderson made their first sortie back to the Soviet Union to garner material evidence. They had specific instructions. Murray was to take the affidavits, and to question witnesses privately. Tomlinson was to take no active part in the proceedings, after affecting introductions. Murray was also to attempt to persuade some of the witnesses to travel to Great Britain to take the stand and give evidence in person. It was a formidable task.

But then, quite a few people still considered the outcome to be a trifle academic. Most of Tomlinson's colleagues – and Tomlinson himself, still in some deep recesses of his mind – could not believe that the affair would go the distance of a court trial. Their case seemed so solid, there was a buoyancy about the defence team. Surely, once Gecas and his people knew that they would be fought to the final bridge, they would realise the futility of their action and quietly retreat.

'Just get the material and get out,' said David Scott before they left. 'Keep it secret, don't let everybody know why you're there. And remember, whatever else happens, you're not there as a journalist. Get the evidence, that's all.'

The three men arrived in a Soviet Union so different from that of 1987 as to be almost unrecognisable. The great communist megalith was crumbling beneath its citizens' feet. Revolutionary change was immediately apparent. Hundreds of delayed passengers thronged Moscow airport. Chaos reigned. People were fighting for baggage, black-market money was being openly touted. The welcome face of Pavel Tsarvoulonov appeared through the crowd. He seized the visitors and hustled them through passport control. Alan Henderson's bag was missing; Murray's suitcase had been broken into. Things unthinkable in the former Soviet Union were happening all about them. Law and order, it seemed, was breaking down before their eyes.

They rushed to Tsarvoulonov's car and drove through the slush and dirty snow of Moscow. 'Only one windscreen?' said Tomlinson. 'Economy drive, Pavel?'

'The others were stolen,' replied the Russian grimly.

Nataliya Kolesnikova, they were assured, was still committed to helping them. 'But you should be aware, there is a problem in Lithuania, and there might be difficulties in Byelorussia.' Tsarvoulonov could not travel with the three Scots; as a journalist he was committed to the unfolding events in Moscow. It was not a promising start.

They booked into an hotel a few hundred yards from the Kremlin, and as they walked through Red Square later that evening gangs of youths began to follow them. They strode quickly towards the protective company of a nearby policeman.

'Why are there so many people on Red Square?' Tomlinson asked the officer.

He turned indifferently away. 'It's how things are these days,' he commented. They returned quickly to their hotel.

They met Nataliya Kolesnikova on 7 January. It was Christmas Day in Russia – the first Christmas Day to be celebrated officially in that country for 73 years. The KGB colonel gave a statement to Len Murray. 'Will you travel to Scotland to give evidence?' he asked.

'Yes,' she replied. 'If I can.'

'What did you mean by "if you could"?' Tomlinson asked her later.

She shook her head slowly, almost helplessly. Things are not what they were. Things are not what they seem.

They returned through the grim streets to their rooms on the 22nd floor of the city-centre hotel. The Kremlin was clearly visible from their windows. Tomlinson looked out towards its byzantine towers. The road below him was vaguely familiar. It had hosted televised triumphal parades of armies, heads of state, astronauts. It was lined with high and stately buildings. He looked again at them, shocked. They were purely, literally, a façade. There was nothing behind their six-foot deep street-fronts. They were like a permanent Hollywood film set. If ever there was evidence of the dissolution of the communist state, this was it: not so much the fact of those deceitful heights of masonry; but that a Westerner was suddenly allowed to see through the fiction, a British journalist was booked into rooms which overlooked the external fabric of the big lie.

On the next morning they moved to Vilnius, capital of the newly insurgent republic of Lithuania. The three scheduled flights had been reduced to one due to a fuel shortage. They checked into the Hotel Lietuva and lodged in their rooms the necessary imported supplies of toilet paper. If such a thing was possible, the Lietuva had deteriorated since 1987. Len Murray looked about him in a state of dulled astonishment. There were now armed guards in the hotel, and all guests had to produce identification before they were allowed in or out of the building. Only one door was open from the foyer to the street. Outside, beggars pleaded on the road. Soviet Lithuania was plainly falling apart. Would it take the Scottish Television defence case down with it?

The three men walked with Kolesnikova from the Hotel Lietuva to the procurator's office, through uncleared snow, past empty shops, fending off mendicants. Groups of angry, argumentative people clustered on street corners, shouting at each other and gesticulating furiously. Half the street lights were out in the gathering dusk. The once crowded, hushed capital of Lithuania appeared suddenly sinister, and they quickened their pace towards the office of Bacucionis.

It was guarded by a dozen armed policemen. They were escorted up to Bacucionis's old room. They waited outside. A hubbub of noise and activity surrounded them: telephones rang and were quickly, heatedly answered, typewriters chattered, people were boxing papers and tying the containers with string. It was like an evacuation. There was a mood of half-controlled panic about the place, an urgency far removed from the slow, quietly mouldering procurator's office of 1987; far removed, indeed, from any atmosphere that Tomlinson had encountered, anywhere.

Sitting at the end of a long table in Bacucionis's former office was a man named Nikolai Nikolayevich Krimpovski. He was the new Soviet procurator in Lithuania. Nataliya Kolesnikova sat demurely and with unusual reticence at the side of the room while Tomlinson told this satrap that he needed to see a number of documents, which had formerly been held in these offices. Krimpovski was courteous and friendly, but as the two men held each other's eyes, talking directly across the table without overt reference to the interpreter, properly if absurdly, as if each of them understood the other's language and the lull between sentences while Henderson translated was a mere social nicety – as they talked quietly it seemed to Tomlinson that an unspoken comprehension passed between them. He knows that I'm in trouble, and I know that he's in trouble. I might be about to lose a court case; he is about to lose a country.

'It is necessary for us to have copies of all of your trial documents. Signed by you, confirmed by you as authentic. And we must see the witnesses Migonis, Aleksynas and Mickevicius without any impediment.'

'I will do everything possible. Is there anything else?'

'We would like to see Mr Bacucionis. We would like a statement from him, and we would like him to go to Britain to testify.'

Krimpovski nodded. 'Okay. There is one problem. They – ' he indicated out of the window in the general, sweeping direction of the Lithuanian independence movement ' – have locked the documents up, and they will not let us in. We will give you everything that we can get.'

He addressed the dozen Russians who stood about the room. They began to talk among themselves. Henderson later explained that they were discussing the awkward problem of recovering state manuscripts from a large group of dedicated separatists without causing too much trouble. Krimpovski got to his feet, and every seated Soviet citizen in the room did the same. Tomlinson stayed in his chair.

'I must have your guarantee,' he said, 'that we will have these documents before we leave.'

Krimpovski placed his huge palms on the table-top and leaned towards the journalist.

'Mr Tomlinson,' he said, 'I will do everything I can to help you. But we have a problem here.'

'I appreciate that. I have a problem in the United Kingdom. If you want the justice that you say you have always sought, you have to help us prove our case.'

As they left the room Krimpovski barked a sentence in their direction.

'You must not speak out loudly,' translated Henderson.

'Where?'

'In the street. Some of them will come back to the hotel with us.'

'I don't want them to come back with us.'

'They are going to, whether you want it or not.'

'To make sure we're okay?'

'I don't know.'

Four of them did so, and the festive atmosphere was continued over dinner that evening. The Scots had been warned not to use English in public, and the Russians were forbidden to speak Russian, so only those who spoke Lithuanian accompanied them to the restaurant. One of the Russians overindulged in brandy, and as they walked back to the hotel through the streets of Vilnius he suddenly said, 'Mr Bob, I am very good at singing Rabbie Burns.'

'Ah. That's great.'

The man checked his stride, and burst into a baritone rendering of 'My Love is Like a Red Red Rose'. It occurred to some of the party that references to red roses – or red anything – in Vilnius in January 1991 might be inflammatory. This was pointed out to the tuneful Russian. He sang louder, and it dawned on Tomlinson that he knew exactly what he was doing. It was fierce bravado; the words ill-feeling no longer applied to relationships between Russians and Lithuanians in Vilnius; they had slid back into an atavistic hatred. And that was of no help whatsoever to the three men from Scottish Television.

Back at the Hotel Lyatova, it seemed as though half of the television news networks in the world were jostling in the bars and corridors, trying to find telephone lines and appropriate power points. They were surrounded by images of a city under seige. And through the fracas wandered a peculiarly innocent group of American schoolchildren, talking excitedly among themselves about prospective visits to the main radio station. 'The revolution's happening,' one of them gleefully told Tomlinson. Fine, thought the only television journalist in Vilnius without a camera crew. At any other time, just fine. Our job is to get evidence for our counsel in the midst of all this.

They stood by the foyer elevator door. A lift descended, the door opened, and out of it stepped a familiar form. It was Misha, the Intourist 'interpreter' who had been unexpectedly imposed upon Tomlinson and the film crew four years earlier.

'Misha! What are you doing here?'

'Bob! I am showing some American students around. What are you doing here?'

'Oh, the usual. Just the old war crimes thing.'

Somebody called out to Misha and he walked hurriedly away.

'Are you here for long?' Tomlinson shouted after him, across the crowded lobby.

The Russian paused. 'Probably another few days.'

'I'll see you later.'

Tomlinson telephoned David Scott from his room. 'We are drinking beer,' he said. 'Severely. There have been some extremely bad developments. Only beer is on offer.'

They travelled to Kaunas to see Motiejus Migonis on the following day, armed with the few documents that the Russians had managed to disinter. They were driven to the enormous housing estate in a minibus with drawn blinds. It stopped on the outskirts of the estate.

'You know where he lives,' said Kolesnikova.

'Wait a minute. Are you not coming with us?'

'Oh, no, no, no. That is impossible.'

'Does he know we're coming?'

'No.'

The interviews are arranged, the Russians had said. All is in order. But the Russians, despite clinging to nominal power over the republic of Lithuania, were clearly no more in control of the place than was Bob Tomlinson. Murray, Henderson and Tomlinson followed the front of a tower block, entered, climbed a flight of stairs and knocked on Migonis's door. One of his sons opened it.

'My father is away, working as a watchman. He will be back at five o'clock.'

'Could you tell him that Bob Tomlinson of Scottish Television called. I'm in this part of the country and . . . I thought I'd stop in to say hello.' It did not sound convincing. 'I'll come back.'

Through the hallway door he could see the whole of Migonis's family standing around a television set, glued to a news broadcast featuring live pictures from the centre of Vilnius.

They went for lunch. 'Do not speak,' warned Madame Kolesnikova as they entered the restaurant. Only three people

in their party of ten spoke Lithuanian; the remainder stayed
silent throughout the meal, while Lithuanian waiters regarded
them suspiciously and a radio blared urgent news from behind
the counter.

They drove to the house of Leonas Mickevicius, and were
again let out a block from his entrance. In the streets crowds of
pedestrians had stopped to listen to transistor radios. 'It's a
ba's up, boys,' said Tomlinson to the others. 'They're a' aff
their heids.' The Russians looked at them blankly. 'These yins
cannae deliver,' the three Scots agreed. They climbed the
rickety staircase to Mickevicius's room. Tomlinson knocked on
the door, it opened, and the journalist put his foot in the crack.

'Bob Tomlinson, Scottish Television. I came to see you
some time ago. I have now brought my lawyer. Can we come
in?'

'Who brought you here?'

'What do you mean?'

'Only the KGB could have brought you here.'

'We have come of our own will. I am very cold, can I
come in?'

'No. Who brought you here?'

'I have been to your house before. We are here on our
own.'

Mickevicius let them in.

'My feet are cold,' said Tomlinson. 'Can I take my welling-
tons off?' He removed the boots, dropped a running tape
recorder into one, and laid them on the floor.

'I am saying nothing,' insisted Leonas Mickevicius, 'other
than what I have said before. The television people lied to me
before – '

'What do you mean, we lied to you? We have never lied
to you. We have only broadcast what you told us.'

'I am saying no more.'

'Do you agree that this is your signature?' asked Len
Murray, producing a statement from the Lithuanian procurator's office.

Mickevicius blinked at the papers. 'The contents are correct,' he said. 'It is true what is written here, and here . . . but the signature on this is so blurred. My glasses do not work.'

'Did you tell me the truth before?' asked Tomlinson.

'Of course I did. But no signature, no signature. I've had enough. I could have gone to Britain, or America, or Brazil, but I didn't go. I thought, well, whatever . . . After the last time people were coming here they had English people with them. And they wanted to string up, they wanted to get Gecevicius.'

'I don't want to string up Gecevicius. I want to defend myself because Gecevicius said I lied.'

'You are not lying. You have got documents.'

'Mr Mickevicius,' said Tomlinson, 'if the court in Scotland ever wanted you to go there, are you too unwell to travel?'

'I suffered a stroke and get terribly giddy.'

As they left Mickevicius said a few words to Alan Henderson. 'One thing,' interpreted Henderson, 'if you see him – Gecevicius – give him regards from me.'

'He's joking.'

Henderson passed on the response, and turned back.

'Yes,' he said.

The three men returned to the minibus in the depressing certainty that a key witness had just deleted his name from their cause. Leonas Mickevicius had served 18 years' imprisonment for his activities in the Second World War; he was taking no more risks. The imminence of a free Lithuania gave him the opportunity to frustrate his former prosecutors, and he was seizing that opportunity with both hands. If the performance of Mickevicius was any kind of an augur, it was beginning to look as if Antanas Gecas might have a case in court.

As they sat in silence before bowls of soup in an otherwise empty restaurant it occurred to Tomlinson that the Muscovites were not just nervous, they were frightened. Murray and

Tomlinson exchanged a few words, and their hosts panicked. 'Sssh, sssh! Be quiet!' they whispered, looking about them with scared expressions. 'Don't say anything!' This situation, mused the Scots dumbly, is desperate.

Luckily, Motiejus Migonis was smiling when he opened his door to them at 7.00 p.m. that evening. Tomlinson listened anxiously as Len Murray put his questions, as Alan Henderson interpreted them, as Migonis replied, and as Henderson rendered his response back into English . . . but Motiejus Migonis held true.

'Yes, that is my signature,' he affirmed of his 1987 statement. 'Yes, my signature is applied to every page.'

'Can you tell me, is what you said in that statement true?'

'What has been said here is the truth.'

Relief washed over Tomlinson.

'Did anyone force you to say these things?' continued Murray.

'That did not happen.'

Slowly, carefully, Motiejus Migonis was led back to his recollections of Slutsk, of the pits there, and of the shootings, and of his platoon commander.

'What I would like to do, Mr Migonis,' said Len Murray, 'is to put my initials on this protocol. Would you be prepared to initial this protocol along with me?'

The tension rose again as the three-way translation took its course.

'Yes,' said Migonis. 'I can do that.' He got up and went to look for a pen, returned and signed the form.

Tomlinson, Murray and Henderson drove back to the Hotel Lyatova, not knowing what to make of the day's events.

They travelled through the deep snow to see Juozas Aleksynas on his tattered smallholding in the plain around Alytus. Two cows and a pig foraged in the frozen earth which surrounded his tumbledown cabin, while inside a log fire strove to keep the bitter cold at bay.

'Could I ask him,' said Len Murray through Alan Henderson, 'about his time with the 2nd Lithuanian Defence Battalion?'

'Ask what you want.'

'I hope I have it right, but I think they were a sort of auxiliary police force to the German occupying forces: is that right?'

Aleksynas replied instantly and with clarity. 'The battalion was founded in 1941,' he said. 'As a battalion for internal purposes. This later proved not to be the case. And I left it, and anything further that I have said already, is the truth.'

'Can he tell me when he left the battalion?'

'Kada isbeges,' corrected Aleksynas. 'When I fled.'

'Yes.'

'I deserted from the battalion in 1942. Spring, probably about the month of May.'

What was the battalion's duty in the area of Minsk? Murray asked Aleksynas.

'The duties of the battalion were transportation of people of Jewish nationality from the towns surrounding Minsk. They were being taken from places like Baranovichi, Kliotsk, Kaidanovo – I do not remember exactly. Gecevicius was in charge of all our operations during this time.'

'And where were they taking the Jewish people to?'

'They took them to pits which had been dug, and shot them in the pits.'

'And was the 2nd Battalion there when this was happening?'

Aleksynas nodded assuredly. 'When the Jews were taken away to be shot the German gendarmerie would go, and the 2nd battalion as well. The gendarmerie would most often form a cordon around the shooting area so that no one could escape, and the order was usually given – Lithuanians to shoot . . . Gecevicius would give the order.'

'He spoke of pits. Can he tell me something of these pits?'

'I could not say for sure, but they were perhaps about two metres across; but as regards length, I could not say. They were long, so long that taking all those people from the towns to shoot them, they were able just to line them up and they would fall in. They would do the same with others so that they would fall on top of the ones who had been previously shot . . . There were lots of little towns round about which we visited to seek out people of Jewish nationality – definitely more than two or three – maybe ten times.'

'These Jewish people,' pressed Murray, 'were they all of the same sex? Men or women or what?'

'All types of people were shot.'

'What about children?'

'They transported everyone, even children.'

'And when they got the children to the pits, what did they do with them?'

'They shot the children, and that was it.'

Not for the first or the last time, Bob Tomlinson experienced a paradoxical twist of emotion: a shameful relief at hearing such terrible testimony; something close to cold pleasure at having his work confirmed by an old man in a dirty shack in a country which was collapsing around his ears. Len Murray continued remorselessly.

'What did the battalion do at Slutsk?'

'The shooting lasted two days in Slutsk. The Jews would be herded into the square. Those who were not to be shot were taken to the synagogue, and the others were taken to the pits which had been prepared.'

'And Gecevicius, where was he?'

'He was in his normal place at all times.'

'Giving orders?'

'He did not leave the area – '

'Then he was commanding?'

'He was commanding – platoon commander.'

'And was he there at the pits?'

'He was there at the pits.'

'And did he give orders at the pits?'

'He would give orders, and sometimes delegate to his second-in-command.'

Juozas Alekysnas agreed that all of his previous statements had been true – 'what I said today is on a smaller scale' – and he too initialled an affidavit for Murray.

Back in Vilnius, the three Scots had continued to work their way through such documents as had been made available to them, such trial transcripts and witness statements as had not fallen into the unco-operative hands of the Lithuanian nationalists. From this chaotic pile of bureaucratic papers, other names emerged: names new to Tomlinson. Somebody called Pocevicius, a man named Goga, another called Garvinas, these and others recurred throughout recent testimony, all obviously able to add to the weight of evidence against Antanas Gecas. They would not, however, manage to see those men in the January of 1991. The dramatic upheaval of contemporary Lithuania suddenly overwhelmed their efforts to trawl through the events of 50 years earlier.

They returned to the Hotel Lietuva after seeing Juozas Aleksynas that Friday afternoon, expecting to catch a train to Minsk on the following Sunday night, having had a weekend off in Vilnius. All three men were tired, and Alan Henderson was running what they thought was an influenza temperature, but which turned out to be sinusitis with complications, and which infected the whole left-hand side of his face. As they entered the hotel building many of the staff were weeping openly. The Soviet army had sent paratroopers into Lithuania to occupy the main administrative centres. The American schoolchildren were excitedly well informed about developments. Alan Henderson translated an announcement on the hotel's intercom, which informed guests that a train between Latvia and Poland had been stopped by the military, and could anybody with food take it to the stranded passengers, so that they would know that it was not the Lithuanians who had broken their journey, but the Soviets.

At 2.00 a.m. on Saturday morning, Tomlinson was woken by an insistent, unfamiliar rumbling noise from the streets outside. He got out of bed and went to the window. Three hundred yards away a large bridge crossed the river close to the Lithuanian parliament building. In the space of a few minutes he counted 50 tanks making their way across the bridge in the company of lorries and armoured cars.

At 10.00 a.m. Tomlinson's room telephone rang. It was Nikolai Nikolayevich Krimpovski. 'Come to my office,' he said. 'At once.'

They hurried through Vilnius, past fires lit by an excited citizenry on the cobblestones, past street-corner orators and thronging crowds, and they made their way through the armed, visored guards to Krimpovski's room. It was 10.30. A guard blocked their way. His finger was on the trigger of an assault rifle. Tomlinson extended his right hand. 'Good morning,' he said. The soldier looked baffled, and then took Tomlinson's hand and shook it. He was trembling. They passed through the ranks.

Krimpovski was sitting at the end of his long table. Procurator Bacucionis and a pale Nataliya Kolesnikova were in chairs in a corner of the room. Krimpovski put his palms on the desk-top and leaned forward.

'Well, Mr Tomlinson,' he said. 'Here are all the documents that you asked us for that we have been able to get. Are you happy with that?'

'Pass them to Alan Henderson,' said Tomlinson. Henderson flicked through them, and nodded assent.

'Yes,' said Tomlinson.

'Have you seen all the people you wanted to see?'

'Yes.'

'Is there anything else that I can do for you?'

'No. You have been very helpful.'

'In that case you leave at 6.00 tonight.'

Tomlinson bridled. 'No we don't. We are not leaving at 6.00 tonight.'

'You leave at 6.00.'

'Nikolai Nikolayevich, we have arranged to travel at 6.00 tomorrow night. We are tired. We are not moving from here before then. We have no reason to leave before then.'

Krimpovski banged the table with his fist. 'You must leave!'

Tomlinson banged his end of the table. 'What are you trying to tell us? What is going to happen? I have seen the tanks. I have seen people in tears. I have seen the people in the streets. What is happening?'

The Russian glared at the three Scots. 'After midnight tonight,' he said, 'I am going to take action. I have the authority to do so and I am going to do it, in order to clear the situation up. After 12.00 tonight I can no longer guarantee your safety. And after that time there will be no more trains out of Vilnius.'

Bob Tomlinson looked across the room at his hosts. 'In that case,' he said, 'we'll leave at 6.00.'

'Good. Be ready with your cases. Someone will knock on your room door. Do not speak. They will come in. They will take your cases and escort you down to cars. Do not speak to them at any time. The hotel bill has been settled. That is it. Thank you.'

'What is going to happen here?' Tomlinson was idling towards the door.

'The situation is getting out of control. Drastic measures must be taken. Law and order must be restored. You will not be safe here in Vilnius, after midnight tonight.'

Television crews from most of the Western world scurried about the foyer of the Hotel Lietuva, anxious for news, for gossip, for leads. 'My God,' thought Tomlinson when they walked back in, 'if only you knew who I'd been with. If only I was on a different brief. I'm on a world exclusive here, but . . .'

He placed an urgent call to Scott in Glasgow. Miraculously, it was connected. 'There's about to be mayhem here,' he said. 'It's a world story, David. Can we not do anything?'

'Remember why you're there. You reporting it isn't going to stop what's going to happen. You are in Lithuania to get information about Gecas. Just get it and get out. What can you do anyway, Bob? You don't have a camera. I'm sorry for you, but you're not in a position to do anything. Just get out, and be careful.'

Tomlinson, Murray and Henderson ate the remainder of their imported supplies for lunch and gave the leftovers to the tearful hotel staff. Suddenly, Murray and Tomlinson looked at each other. 'What about the American schoolkids?'

They were in the foyer, a cluster of loud and gregarious youngsters of 17 and 18 years old, swapping stories about tanks and paratroopers. 'Where are your teachers?' asked Tomlinson. They were produced, along with the interpreter Misha. 'You must come to my room,' said Tomlinson. 'Now.' He looked at Misha. Misha had been Intourist. Misha had therefore almost certainly been an employee of the KGB. 'Just the teachers, please,' said Tomlinson.

'Look,' he continued in the comparative security of his hotel room, 'it does not matter how we came to know this, but you have to believe that we have impeccable information. The Soviet army is going to start firing in anger here later on tonight. And the trains will be stopped. How are you planning on travelling?'

The American teachers looked at him aghast. 'We were going by train to Riga.'

'Not any more. You must get a bus, and go now.'

The teachers looked almost ready to disbelieve this strange Scot with his fantastical source of information.

'If you do not do as I say, you may be locked up in this city for a very long time. It will not be a pleasant place to holiday.'

Tomlinson could hardly believe his own words. He had revisited the Soviet Union to help collect routine material for the defence of a libel case, and found himself trying to help

American schoolchildren escape from a revolution. He then called for Misha.

'It does not matter which party you belong to now,' said Tomlinson privately to his former interpreter. 'I don't care whether you believe in Soviet control or in Lithuanian freedom. I'm telling you, for the safety of those schoolchildren you must get them out of here.'

Misha looked distraught. 'How do you know this?'

'It doesn't matter. Get them out, tonight.'

The teachers and their charges left Vilnius by bus that night. On the following day the Red Army's tanks killed nine Lithuanian civilians, and its feeble hold over the hearts and minds of the people of the Baltic states was fractured beyond repair. Mikhail Gorbachev's tragic attempt to hold the Soviet Union together in the face of irresistible change was doomed by the bloody events of that weekend in the republic where, 50 years earlier, Antanas Gecevicius had joined a police battalion formed and commanded by the Third Reich. And the very men and women who had helped Scottish Television to prepare its case against exiled war criminals were now conspiring to murder civilians.

Alan Henderson seemed dangerously ill as they waited that evening for the men to come and escort them out of the danger zone. No Soviet medications had helped him, he had grown hourly more weak, and by 6.00 he had lost his voice – which was an unfortunate affliction for their only interpreter.

At 6.00 there was a knock on the door. Feeling vaguely foolish, Tomlinson and Murray said nothing. The door opened and four huge men wearing leather jackets walked in, nodded, picked up their bags, and walked out again, signalling with their heads that they should be followed. Astonishingly, the lift on the landing of the Hotel Lietuva – which was usually an evasive creature – was waiting, open. Their keys were silently taken by one of the Russians, and they left without checking out. A limousine was waiting by the kerb. Nataliya Kolesnikova was sitting in its front passenger seat. The driver accelerated

furiously away from the Hotel Lietuva and out of Vilnius, and
as they left the dark and brooding city the streets were lined
with people carrying placards, all marching in the same direction: the opposite direction to the one being taken by their
speeding automobile. They were marching towards the parliament building and its ring of tanks. At midnight, thought
Tomlinson bitterly. At midnight.

He would read later that Gorbachev claimed to have
known nothing in advance of the night assault on the Lithuanian demonstrators, and he hated the lie. Bob Tomlinson had
known about it. Len Murray and Alan Henderson had known
about it. There was nothing unpremeditated about that attack.
Three Scottish castaways had been informed 14 hours before
. . . but not the General Secretary of the Communist Party
which commanded Krimpovski? Not the President of the
USSR?

They drove to the border between Lithuania and
Byelorussia.

As the winter of 1991 turned into spring and summer, as the
War Crimes Bill went through its final convoluted motions and
became an Act, as the press speculated wildly about the kind
of forms that war-crimes trials in Great Britain might take –
mini-Nuremburgs, enlivened by high-technology, some newspapers suggested, with rows of ancient men in the witness box
being quizzed through satellite television links by prosecutors
and witnesses from the other side of the world – Scottish
Television's own mini-Nuremburg made its slow, inexorable
way towards the courtroom of Edinburgh.

Others were also at work. On 26 September the *Independent* reported that:

> Britain's first Nazi war-crimes trial moved a stage nearer at the
> weekend when a team of police and investigators flew to
> Moscow to investigate claims against a suspected mass mur-
> derer now living in Scotland . . .

Lothian Police in Edinburgh have set up a specialist unit to investigate suspects in Scotland, and it is members of this squad who have flown to the Soviet Union. England and Scotland have separate judicial systems, so Scottish suspects cannot be investigated by the much larger specialist team of police and researchers which has been appointed for the rest of Britain under the Metropolitan Police.

It is believed that the team from Scotland will concentrate its inquiries on a former Lithuanian who served as a junior lieutenant in the 12th battalion of the Lithuanian Security Police, which participated in the mass murder of Jews in Kaunas, Lithuania, and Slutsk, Minsk, Dukara and Kaidanov in Byelorussia.

They are expected to examine Soviet archives in Moscow, and to interview witnesses in the areas of the mass killings.

The suspect is one of several men investigated by a commission of inquiry set up by the Home Office in 1987 to investigate evidence against suspected Nazis in Britain. It is understood he was one of the three which the authors of the report, Sir Thomas Hetherington, former director of public prosecutions, and William Chalmers, former crown agent (the equivalent for Scotland), decided could be prosecuted on the basis of the evidence they had seen.

For any trials to go ahead, the police have to submit a file to the present crown agent or DPP, for him to decide whether there is sufficient evidence for a trial . . . In view of the fact that suspects and witnesses to events 50 years ago are now mostly in their 70s and 80s, the War Crimes Act abolished the lengthy committal procedure used for normal trials of serious crimes, so that once a decision to prosecute was taken, it would theoretically be possible to move to a trial within a few weeks.

In October 1991 Bob Tomlinson and Alan Henderson were sent back yet again, hot on the heels of the Lothian and Borders Police Special Unit, to a Lithuania still writhing under vestigial Soviet rule. It was planned as a short, almost negligible visit, to reconfirm witnesses and to drum up any fresh evidence that might have become available since January, to keep the defence's pot simmering.

Tomlinson telephoned Pavel Tsarvoulonov before leaving. 'I want to meet Madame Kolesnikova once more,' he
said. 'And Messrs Bacucionis, Migonis, Aleksynas, Mickevicius. We have to go through more documentation, check
statements . . . not quite the whole thing again, Pavel, but
almost.'

'Bob,' said Tsarvoulonov, 'things are changing very
quickly here. You know that Lithuania is breaking free of the
revolution. President Gorbachev is having trouble with them.
You had better move fast.'

Tomlinson did not yet fully understand the need for
hurry. So far as he could see, Migonis, Aleksynas and Mickevicius were going nowhere. No revolution would affect them,
surely?

Tomlinson and Henderson met with Nataliya Kolesnikova
upon their arrival in Moscow. The city was more fraught and
nerve-wracked than ever; a place in political turmoil, with
loudly spoken criticisms of the Communist Party and of
Mikhail Gorbachev echoing from groups of people gathered on
every corner, or huddled around television sets. Moscow was
agitated, its streets were busy to the point of frenzy. Suddenly,
it looked like a capital in which anything could happen. For
the Russians, after 70 years that was certainly an exhilarating
experience. For the three Scots, it was simply, selfishly
unnerving.

Even that haven of official calm, Colonel Kolesnikova's
offices, were now as lively as a Saturday fair. People came and
went from the room as they talked, disrespectful of the old
order of things. Kolesnikova agreed to help them find new and
old documentation, and to see if witnesses could be prevailed
upon to travel to Scotland. But there was a new unease about
this gracious woman, and the Scots' worry intensified.

The Moscow hotels had also changed. They now offered
room service. Tomlinson availed himself of this new luxury by
ordering scrambled eggs and toast on his first morning. He
lifted the lid of the salver and two large cockroaches stared

unblinkingly up at him. Was this some joke? Was this an omen?

They travelled to Vilnius with Nataliya Kolesnikova. 'We will need to see the new procurator,' she had commented, worryingly. Where was Bacucionis? The Hotel Lietuva was busier than at any time in its stricken existence. Television crews still thronged its corridors and jostled in its bars. They were met at the procurator's office by a young man named Vydmantis Viskaukas. Alan Henderson had already met Viskaukas during his work with the Crown Office unit, and he effected the introductions.

'This is very important to us,' Tomlinson told the Lithuanian. 'We are being sued for a lot of money by Gecevicius. Can we meet Bacucionis?'

Viskaukas shrugged his shoulders, as if to say, if you must, you must. It's up to you. Then he took them into an adjacent building. There were policemen on every landing. Bacucionis was there.

'Unfortunately,' he told them, 'I have been removed from my position as chief procurator. But I will do what I can for you.' He dropped his voice. 'I will make a telephone call for you,' he whispered.

'What about the documents?'

The man that Tomlinson had known three years earlier as a cheerful, brash character shrugged helplessly. 'The other side have the documents,' he said. Alan Henderson indicated silence to Tomlinson. 'Leave it with me,' said Bacucionis finally. They went out again into the snow and the police-lined streets.

'What was that about?' asked Tomlinson.

'Bacucionis was KGB and a Communist Party member,' said Henderson. 'He has been removed. He is under very heavy pressure. Vydmantis is now the key to this.'

It was an inauspicious start. Nobody would promise to arrange meetings or to gather documents, half of which were reportedly in the one building, and the other half locked away in another. 'If' was their constant refrain: if we can, we will; if the papers are there; if it is possible. Something was happening in Lithuania that Tomlinson could not understand. A massive sea change was underway which looked capable of overturning both the imposed government of 50 years, and as a minor incidental, of sweeping aside his once unassailable defence against a suit of defamation in an Edinburgh court.

'Would you come to dinner?' he asked Viskaukas. 'Tonight, at the Lietuva?'

The new procurator agreed. They met in the Black Bar, with vodka and duty-free whisky. They discussed the weather, and they complimented each other on their national drinks. They skirted the political situation like dogs around a fire. They ate the new national haute cuisine: beefburger and chips. They went up to Tomlinson's room, uncorked another bottle and cracked open cans of beer.

'I am concerned,' said Tomlinson finally to Vydmantis Viskaukas. 'Nobody seems to know quite where all the documents now are. They are crucial to me. We need the transcripts of the Plunge and other trials, where our man was named. All I get is "perhaps", "maybe", and "if".' He paused. 'Gecevicius,' he continued, 'is suing us. We are going to win.'

Viskaukas's reply was disturbing.

'Well,' he said. 'Hopefully you will win. I have met the Scottish police, and hopefully they too will be successful. I believe they may have a case. But there are problems.'

'What problems?'

'There is a political change happening here. Things are in turmoil.'

And that was all that the new procurator would say. They arranged that on the following day they would have access to some documents, and would then travel to see the three putative witnesses. The moment Viskaukas left the room Tomlinson placed a call to David Scott. He finally reached him at home in the early hours of the morning.

'It's beer again,' said Tomlinson. 'Lots of it.'

The producer sighed. 'I'll see you when you get back,' he said.

They travelled to see Motiejus Migonis. He confirmed what he had previously told them, but with a new, perceptible reticence.

'Has anybody else been to see you?' asked Tomlinson.

The old man nodded. 'Yes, of course. But . . . I will stand by everything I have told the British police.'

'What do you mean, the British police?'

He turned out to be referring to Sir Thomas Hetherington and William Chalmers, who had visited him and videotaped his testimony during their investigations for the Home Secretary a few months earlier.

They went to see the intransigent Mickevicius.

'I am saying nothing more,' he said, 'than what I have already said to your British police.'

'Which police?'

'I said it all on camera.' The diligent Hetherington and Chalmers again. The Lithuanians obviously had those two eminent lawyers placed as top guns in the Westminster KGB.

It was by then too late to go to Alytus to see Aleksynas, so the small party returned to Vilnius. Tomlinson telephoned Scott.

'Things are looking better.' Not quite champagne, but better.

'There's something else,' Scott said. 'A British journalist's thinking of writing a book on the whole affair. She's been to Lithuania. She tells me our witnesses have turned.'

They went to see Aleksynas in his house, without any of the earlier precautions of meeting him in the police station of that controlled area.

'Have you seen any British journalists?'

'Yes.' He produced an empty bottle of Scotch whisky. It looked as incongruous in that shack on a smallholding on the Eastern European plains as a samovar in a Glasgow tenement.

These people, thought Tomlinson, are getting more British visitors than Disneyland. Aleksynas's son and daughter-in-law had recently been killed in a car crash, and he was looking after his two grandchildren. He affirmed that he was prepared to repeat his evidence.

For all the reticent confirmations that at least two witnesses would stand solid, the defence case was clearly in danger. Too many people were chasing too few old, nervous men, too much pressure was being applied on them to restate the misdeeds that they would sooner have forgotten. The slackening of the iron grip of the KGB on Lithuania, welcome as that was, would ironically only damage Scottish Television's chances of keeping their witnesses intact. Would not those witnesses seize the opportunity offered by an independent Lithuania to break for freedom from inquisitive foreign journalists? Might a curious by-product of the collapse of the Soviet Union, be the collapse also of valid legal cases against war criminals in Great Britain?

And even if they agreed to testify, according to what they had told Hetherington and Chalmers – what had they told Hetherington and Chalmers? How much use was that to Scottish Television? How did it differ from their words of three years earlier? How much was now missing?

They returned to Moscow and then to Scotland, and Tomlinson wrote a sombre report for David Scott. The lawyers were called together. Peter Watson was insistent that only one course of action could now be followed. More affidavits must be taken from more witnesses. There was no time to lose. They would begin in Israel.

10

If all of their explorations of the Lithuanian past and the Lithuanian present had been journeys to the heart of darkness, the visit made to Israel by Len Murray and Bob Tomlinson in December 1991 – the visit to the survivors of the round-ups, execution squads and the lime-pits – seemed like a time out of evil, a brief period spent in sunlight and hospitality in the gentle company of those who had lived to tell their story.

The defence team consulted the historian of the holocaust and consultant to the British All-Party War Crimes Group, Dr David Cesarani. They were looking in Israel not only for first-hand remembered accounts of mass murder, but also for individuals whose studies had given them a broad historical perspective on events in Eastern Europe. It had become clear to the journalists involved in the case that to mount a proper defence in a court of law, a wider spectrum of information would be required than that which simply covered the deeds and personnel of the 2nd/12th Lithuanian Auxiliaries. To satisfy a judge, they must effectively tell and retell the whole long story of the destruction of the Lithuanian and Byelorussian Jews, and recount the available biographies of the people responsible – before Slutsk, during Slutsk, after Slutsk, and in all of the thousands of villages and cities which mirrored what had happened at Slutsk. If the essence of television journalism was the efficient and economic reduction of a story to its basic detail, the essence of a legal defence case was apparently the

very opposite: an expansive and logical exposition of the full
tale, losing no vital detail, however small, omitting no educa-
tive reference, leaving out no corroborative statement. Enter-
tainment value was irrelevant to a court of law. Nobody was
going to switch off. You had a captive audience. That was the
law. That was the territory of Len Murray and Peter Watson.
It was a different ball game.

Tomlinson also telephoned Ephraim Zuroff at the Simon
Weisenthal Centre in Jerusalem before he and Murray caught
their flight to Israel ten days before Christmas 1991. They
stayed in the Larome Hotel overlooking the city of Jerusalem,
and on a hot December day in the Middle East, they took their
first statement from Zuroff.

'Antanas Gecas first came to my attention in 1982,'
explained Ephraim Zuroff. He had been at the time a 34-year-
old researcher with the United States Justice Department's
Office of Special Investigations. He had earlier been investigating the case of Jurgis Juodis, the other lieutenant in the 12th
Lithuanian Battalion who had fled down the Ratline, in his
case to the USA.

'The United States began proceedings against him
[Juodis],' said Zuroff, 'basically to strip him of his US citizenship. Those proceedings were based upon the fact that he had
illegally procured his immigration and his citizenship. He had
got into the United States on his declaration that he had never
committed a crime of moral turpitude.

'When his involvement with the 12th Lithuanian Police
Battalion came to our attention then the US authorities began
proceedings in the district court of Mid-Florida against him.
He died before the proceedings could come to a hearing.'

Six other former members of the 12th Battalion had been
indicted in the USA, affirmed Zuroff. And it was, of course, in
the pursuit of a case against them that the name of Antanas
Gecas had arisen, and that other OSI investigator, Neal Sher,
had been sent to Edinburgh in 1982 to conduct the interview
which, five years afterwards, resulted in Gecas's name being

on that seminal list of 17 which was issued from Los Angeles, which in turn led Tomlinson and his television crew through the killing fields of Lithuania and Byelorussia. The jigsaw was closing together, each small piece edging it nearer to a comprehensible canvas.

The two men left Zuroff to see another resident of Jerusalem, Professor Dov Levin, in Yad Vashem, the city's Holocaust Centre. Levin was born in Kaunas, Lithuania, in 1925. 'I was only 16 when war broke out and the Germans came,' this softly spoken old academic told Murray and Tomlinson. 'Even before they came, however, there was considerable trouble in Lithuania. An organisation known as LAF [the Lithuanian Activists' Front], which was an extreme right-wing organisation of Lithuanians with Nazi sympathies, had been distributing posters and handbills in advance that said things like: "If you don't want to be killed, then kill at least one Jew." This stirred up considerable hatred in the local population against the Jewish population in Kaunas.

'My family were the victims of Lithuanian mobs. The Germans came between 22 and 24 June 1941, and they took over the country very quickly. In advance of them, however, armed gangs of Lithuanians were going about. They were without uniform but they were very organised. They were armed with rifles and I remember on I think three occasions my family was taken away by crowds such as I have described. We were asked questions and eventually returned to our homes, but always when we got back we found that we had been robbed. There was always one person in charge of them who would give the commands. They would take the people concerned to fortresses around Kaunas.'

Levin's father, his mother, and his twin sister all died during the holocaust; the first after deportation to Estonia, and the two women in the little-known Polish concentration camp of Stutthof, 20 miles east of Danzig. The teenage Levin stayed in Lithuania, working for the partisan underground, and that is how he came to know more fully of the events which took

place at those nightmarish fortresses which ring the city of
Kaunas. Hearing his story took Tomlinson back to the single
searchlight creaking in the tireless wind, to the empty plains,
the deathly hush of the approach roads, and the old walls
pockmarked with machine-gun bullets.

'Various people have told me,' said Professor Levin in
Jerusalem, 'about the murders at the Seventh and the Ninth
forts. I personally did not see them, but I did have very
convincing evidence . . . The Lithuanian guards who marched
them off to the forts were wearing uniforms and carrying rifles
and bayonets. While I did not see anyone being shot, we
constantly heard shots coming from the direction of the forts.
Sometimes it would be single, individual shots, and other
times continuous shooting. The ghetto was situated about four
miles from the forts.

'My grandfather and his wife, my two uncles, aunts and
their families were taken in one of the "aktions" in September
1941 to the Ninth Fort. These "aktions" were moves against
the Jewish population. They were marched off by Lithuanians
in the direction of the forts . . . When these "aktions" were
carried out several hundred were taken at a time. My relatives
were shot either on their first or second night at the fort.

'I remember,' the old man continued, 'one particular girl
called Ela Wolpe who was about 17 at the time. She was taken
to the Seventh Fort but she survived. When the Lithuanians
came into the fort some of the women round about her had
put earth on her face. This made her unattractive, and she was
not touched. Many of the girls taken there had been raped
before they were shot, and most of them of course did not
come back.

'Sometimes there would be a German NCO present, but
usually all the work was being done by armed Lithuanian
battalions. If it is suggested that the 12th Battalion of Lithuanians did not carry out any killings but were only involved in
policing duties, then I would say it is a lie. It is a lie that is very
easy to tell, and it is a common lie . . .

'The battalions of Lithuanians of course were highly mobile and as far as I understand they were frequently moved from place to place by the military command. It was something of a trick on the part of the Germans to get others to do their dirty work, and so it proved in Lithuania. This, incidentally, was a point that was made at the Nuremburg trials, and is not seriously contested.'

Dov Levin arrived in Israel immediately after the war, in 1945. He was not alone among the survivors of the Lithuanian Jews. Tomlinson and Murray knocked next on the door of Ambassador Aba Gefen, who as a young man in Lithuania had kept a diary between the years of 1941 and 1944. His diary was later published under the title *Hope in Darkness*. He was the chairman of the Association of Lithuanian Jews in Israel.

These were brave and gentle men. The dignity of their bearing and the quiet clarity of their testament stood in stark contrast to the evil which had been visited on their younger days. Where Aba Gefen had found hope in the darkness of the early 1940s, the visiting Scots drew strength and courage from his company in the bright Jerusalem winter of 1991. Oranges and lemons hung from the trees beyond his window, and evergreen leaves shone in the sun, and it was again difficult at times to reconcile the calm civilisation of their present surroundings with the tales of barbarism that had to be told. But the stories were related nonetheless, with precision and devotion to detail, as though anything else would only betray the dead.

'I have to say immediately,' commenced Aba Gefen, 'that the killing of Jews in Lithuania began before the Germans arrived. The great majority of atrocities in Lithuania were committed against the Jewish population by Lithuanians under the supervision of Germans. It began on 22 June 1941, when the Germans bombed Kaunas. In a radio broadcast the commander of the Lithuanian Activists' Front – which was actually formed before the Germans came in and prepared to give the invading Germans a joyous welcome – announced that Jews

were shooting at the German troops, and warned that for
every German soldier shot, 100 Jews would be put to death.
That triggered off a wave of violence against the Jewish
population . . . I know from my own experience that those
people whom I describe as pro-Nazi partisans in my diary,
were members of the LAF, of which Gecas was a member.'

Tomlinson and Murray listened quietly, spellbound.
Another large jigsaw piece slotted smoothly into place.

'Those people were conducting the killing of the Jews,'
continued Gefen, 'and they carried out the most horrible
massacres even before the Germans entered Kaunas. They
attacked the suburb of Slabodka, forced a group of Jews to
dance, to recite Hebrew prayers and sing the communist
Internationale. When the sadists tired of their games they
ordered the Jews to kneel, and shot them in the back. Then
they marched down the streets, broke into Jewish houses and
slashed the inhabitants to death. Rabbi Zalman Ossovsky was
found bent over his bloodsoaked books while his severed head
lay in another room . . .

'Those [LAF] activists – among whom Gecas was in the
capacity of an officer – murdered the Jews in the Fourth,
Seventh and Ninth forts in Kaunas and brought death wherever they went . . . A state of mind was being prepared in
which the Jews could be butchered without hindrance, in
accomplishment of a preconceived plan. The victim was tor-
tured until his senses and his human image were lost and,
with no strength to resist any longer, even spiritually, he could
be led to the slaughter. That,' said Ambassador Gefen, 'is how
my parents and two brothers were murdered.'

They left Aba Gefen and took a two-day break which
spanned the Jewish Sabbath. They drove to Bethlehem. There,
a few days before the 1991st commemoration of His birth, they
visited the cradle of Christianity. There, in a Jewish state, they
pondered what Christians had done to their Hebrew neighbours down through the centuries. It was a disturbing juxta-

position of thoughts and impressions: the miracle of the virgin birth, and the horror of the purpose of their mission to its site.

Talking each other back to sanity, they went to take a final testimony from the distinguished historian Shmuel Spector, the world's acknowledged leading authority on the composition and activities of the Nazi Einsatzgruppen and Sonderkommandos in Eastern Europe in the Second World War. Dr Spector gave a lengthy verbal treatise on the precise movements of the groups involving Antanas Gecas. Then, 'I am told,' he said, 'that Gecas alleges that his group were simply involved in guarding railways. I can say that is not true. I am quite sure that there was a separate security force which was charged with the duty of looking after railways, and I am quite sure that an auxiliary police battalion would not have been used for that purpose.

'The local police units were organised in the first hours of German occupation by local nationalistic and pro-Nazi elements. They were welcomed by the Wehrmacht commanders. Later, after being cleared by the SD [the intelligence service of the SS], they were organised into auxiliary police battalions.'

And we know what job those auxiliary police battalions were detailed to carry out, Murray and Tomlinson told each other as they caught a flight back to Britain. Just how much will it take to convince a court of law?

More from Lithuania, was the answer. But what would they find there on yet another visit? How many witnesses would still be singing the same tune?

11

Time was not on their side. Brian Gill QC and Gerry Moynihan, who had been lined up as counsel by Scottish Television, were burdened by other commitments, and by September 1991 it was obvious that another counsel must be found. On 3 September Scottish Television asked Lord Penrose in the Court of Session to have the trial, which had been set for December 1991, postponed for two months. The judge agreed, despite accusations from Antanas Gecas's man in court, John Simpson, that the television company was engaged in a 'deliberately orchestrated attempt to delay the case'. The fresh proof date was set for 11 February 1992.

Colin Campbell QC was brought in as Scottish Television's new counsel, with the advocate Richard Keen as his junior. Peter Watson recommended Campbell, having worked with him on cases arising out of the Piper Alpha oil-rig disaster, and recognised in him at least one quality essential to counsel in the Gecas case: the ability to master great quantities of documentation. It would not be a case for Perry Mason, where the whole event would turn on one shaft of genius, one inspired question and one damning answer. This case must be built, brick by brick, into a compelling edifice of evidence. Watson was equally delighted with the availability of Richard Keen, one of the most effective counsel at the Scottish Bar. Gaining the two of them seemed a rare piece of luck.

Their new counsel promptly told Scottish Television that

they did not, at present, have much of a case. They brought with them a 12-page account of all that needed to be done. It made frightening reading. On 11 December, with the days ticking away, Peter Watson wrote to John Innes at Dundas & Wilson. 'Personally speaking,' he said, 'I am not unhappy with the detail which is being demanded of us, given the dangers which are always inherent in actions of this type.'

But the demands of Campbell and Keen, sensible and well advised as they might be, still added up to a lot more shovelling, with Christmas and Hogmanay looming. Still, as Watson told himself and as he continued in his letter to Innes: 'It is unthinkable that someone such as Gecas should succeed against Scottish Television given what is known about his previous exploits.' Unthinkable, but . . .

'Quite clearly,' concluded Watson, 'there is an enormous amount of work which will require to be done, and done in a very short time.' In private, the young lawyer considered that their task was no longer difficult: it was bordering on the impossible.

On 12 December, on the very afternoon that Murray and Tomlinson, in Israel, were hearing Dov Levin's testimony, Watson met with John Innes at Dundas & Wilson's George Street offices in Edinburgh. Watson came away with a minute of an agreed 24 essential tasks. Several of them could not be completed, he recognised, without a further trip to Lithuania . . . and that was even supposing that a Scottish court could also be persuaded to travel there in February. It was agreed that the final cost to Scottish Television and its insurers could be as much as £200,000. In reality, by the end of the court action it was more than £500,000.

Watson got to work. Tomlinson and Murray flew back into Scotland from Israel on 16 December 1991 to see a *Glasgow Herald* story headlined PLEA TO HOLD LIBEL ACTION IN LITHU-ANIA. 'Lord Milligan,' it read, 'has been approached in the Court of Session by lawyers representing [Scottish Television] to consider an unprecedented overseas sitting to hear evidence

in the case brought by Mr Anton Gecas . . . It is understood
that assurances of security and approval from the Lithuanian
government have been sought and that the Court of Session
will decide this week whether to sit in Lithuania.'

Two days later Lord Milligan acceded, and the press –
which was never to be malnourished by the affair of Scottish
Television and Antanas Gecas – had another field day. HIS-
TORIC MOVE TO LITHUANIA, read one headline; TV WAR CLAIM
CASE TWIST, said another; SCOTS LEGAL FIRST . . . 'Mr Colin
Campbell QC,' followed up the Glasgow Herald, 'counsel for
Scottish Television, told the judge that provisional travel and
accommodation arrangements had been made for the trip.'

Lord Milligan, thought Tomlinson wrily, is about to
experience the joys of the Hotel Lietuva. Must remember to
bring toilet paper. Hell, must remember toilets seats . . .

'The plan,' continued the Glasgow Herald excitedly, 'was
for each side to send two counsel and one solicitor. The
travelling party would also include the judge, Lord Milligan,
who is due to hear evidence in the case in the Court of Session
immediately following the trip to Vilnius, and a shorthand
writer who will also act as clerk of the court . . . officials at the
Court of Session cannot recall a previous example of a judge
travelling outside the UK.'

It was all good, fast, crowd-pleasing stuff, but for the
defence team it only brought home even more starkly the
imminence of their date with judgement – Vilnius, Lithuania,
on 11 February 1992. Precisely two months away.

Letters and faxes were broadcast from Levy & McRae like
confetti, to New York, to Sydney, to Israel, anywhere in the
world where extra information might be gleaned, witnesses
uncovered or that possibly crucial nugget of unknown material
be found which may swing a court case. A firm of solicitors in
Germany proved extremely helpful in tracking down the
evidence given at certain war-crimes trials there. Relevant
information from the extensive files of the OSI in America had
to be found, sieved through and logged. Dundas & Wilson

had brought on board another solicitor, named Graham Fordyce, so stretched were the two Scottish law firms involved in
the case. Trial documents, identified and researched by Tomlinson, Murray and Henderson, had to be reconfirmed; statements assessed for value; witnesses chased up – always,
witnesses to be chased up. Those who could not testify
through ill-health had to be persuaded to hand over medical
certificates; those who had died had to be represented by death
certificates; those, like Mickevicius, who were patently unwilling to take the stand, had to be approached again; those who
might speak had to be preserved from illness and peer-group
pressure.

And the whole convoluted story must be put into its
historical perspective by expert historical evidence. The full
tragedy of the forgotten holocaust of 1941 had to be told to a
Scottish court, before there was a chance of establishing the
role played in it by a young lieutenant named Antanas Gecevicius. It was becoming a 24-hour task. To Peter Watson, the
enormity of the job in hand was eased only slightly by the
realisation that he may never in the remainder of his professional career deal with a bigger or more important case of
law. He had wanted 'high-octane law'; he was getting it – and
along with it came the sort of pressure that he realised Len
Murray must have lived with for decades before he arrived on
the scene fresh-faced and longing for action. The smallest
bonuses, in such a hothouse, caused immeasurable delight.
The sun shone briefly on his work when he was able to confirm
that Federal Express had an office in Vilnius. There would at
least be contact with the Western communications system.
What joy!

Bright sunrises were invariably followed by gloomy
dusks. German witnesses who one day seemed likely to be
able to identify the activities of the 12th Lithuanian Battalion
suddenly had heart attacks, or proved unwilling to testify, or
lost their private documents. Evidence from earlier trials
turned out not to have been given on oath. Four steps forward,

four steps back. And the calendar turned, day after remorseless
day. A report arrived from Lithuania saying that no useful
official in the country would be available to speak to the
defence until, at the earliest, five weeks before the commencement of the trial. Political difficulties and the advent of
Christmas made it impossible. A fax turned up from the
Australian Special Investigations Unit into war crimes, regret-
fully informing Watson that most of that body's information
about the 12th Lithuanian Battalion had come from the British
government's inquiry conducted by Thomas Hetherington and
William Chalmers.

And the Crown – which had cheerfully acknowledged the
help of Scottish Television with its own inquiries in happier
times – was now unable to co-operate. The Crown Agent,
Duncan Lowe, responded in December to a request for an
intervention on the grounds that they were themselves pursuing inquiries into Antanas Gecas, and for any helpful information which may have been gained by the Crown's teams of
state investigators. It could have been, at the least, a useful
source, and the governmental agencies of other countries were
assisting where they could . . . but 'I have now had the
opportunity to discuss the matter with the Lord Advocate,'
replied William Chalmers's successor. '. . . In all the circumstances the Crown cannot intervene in a civil action, even
where the action relates to the same subject matter as concerns
our own ongoing criminal investigations. We have of course
been monitoring closely the course of the civil proceedings and
we have regularly considered the question of the Crown's
intervention . . . The Lord Advocate has also considered your
recent request for information. You will appreciate that in the
normal course of events it would be most unusual to accede to
such a request. The Lord Advocate does not consider that the
unusual circumstances which apply here justify a departure
from the normal course. We would therefore regard it as
quite wrong to supply material from the Crown's confidential

inquiries to parties in a civil action . . . A meeting does not seem worth while.'

Desperation was in the air. The deadline for the defence to lodge documents with the court was 14 January 1992. They ringed the earth with faxes and telephone calls, 24 hours a day as the Christmas and New Year holiday drew closer, but with few practical results. The onus of proof in this as in any other defamation case lay on the defender. Scottish Television had, therefore, to do what no British government had ever done: it had effectively to mount a prosecution of Antanas Gecas, and prove him a war criminal. Bob Tomlinson's outburst at that legal meeting months earlier, that they were in fact planning the first-ever war-crimes trial in Great Britain, was substantially correct.

The burden was great: not only corporate and individual reputations stood to be lost in this hearing; not only large sums of insurers' money; but also the whole momentum which had been set in motion by Scottish Television early in 1987, the movement towards a proper legal consideration of crimes of war in British criminal courts. For, if Scottish Television failed against Antanas Gecas in the civil arena, would the state ever pick up the baton? Would the slate recording Britain's shameful past ever be wiped clean?

It did not help morale when the US Justice Department's Office of Special Investigations replied to requests for some of their boundless reservoirs of information by politely saying that the Crown Office had been given everything they had. Scottish Television should wander down there and borrow it from them. Catch 22. 'The Crown Office,' Watson delicately responded to the Americans, 'no matter how sympathetic they may or may not be, will not and cannot divulge their information to us . . . the same prohibition does not apply to our sharing information with them. It would be our intention to ensure that they had the benefit of all information that we had gathered. It is also fair to note that the Crown Office are closely monitoring our investigations and are seeking to obtain as much benefit as possible from the steps we are taking.

'There appears,' concluded Watson to the OSI, 'to be an overwhelming body of evidence which suggests the involvement of Antanas Gecas in war crimes. The difficulty is simply in gathering the information which exists in many parts of the world in a format acceptable to the courts in Scotland and in the time-frame that we are operating within. It would clearly be a moral outrage if Antanas Gecas is a war criminal, and if he were able to gain substantial monetary damages against Scottish Television as a result of an onus of proof which is placed upon the defender in an action of defamation which could not be discharged in this instance because evidence was either withheld or refused for some particular administrative reason.'

The complications brought about by the once-welcome governmental investigations were at times difficult to bear. Even Alan Henderson, the Glasgow-based interpreter who had been hired by the Crown Office after Scottish Television had first used his services in Lithuania, could now only be employed by Scottish Television, said the Crown, on a strictly impartial basis. He was not to appear involved. The Crown could not be seen to be taking sides. On Christmas Eve David Scott wrote personally to Duncan Lowe, the Crown Agent in Edinburgh. 'You say the Lord Advocate . . . doesn't consider the circumstances sufficiently unusual to justify the departure from the normal course,' said the producer. 'However, we are not dealing with the normal course . . . The War Crimes Inquiry has required various witnesses to sign the Official Secrets Act. This is hindering the preparation of our defence.' At least one prospective witness – a German with evidence about the 12th Lithuanian Battalion – had, when approached by Scottish Television's lawyers, explained that he had signed the Official Secrets Act while collaborating with the British government's confidential inquiries, and therefore, while he was willing to assist Scottish Television, he felt that he was not able to do so.

'If you were to give him permission in writing,' said Scott, 'he would be quite happy to co-operate . . . I am aware of your criminal investigations into Antanas Gecas and would not wish to impede this in any way. Similarly, we would not wish our defence to be impeded by the Crown preventing witnesses from assisting us or appearing on our behalf.'

Duncan Lowe replied quickly, pointedly addressing his letter to Dundas & Wilson. 'I would have thought that it was quite obvious that we cannot align ourselves with a party to a civil action . . . On the other hand, where there are specific matters known to you . . . and individual witnesses who have been instructed by us then there can be no objection to your seeking their assistance. What would be objectionable would be your approaching them [concerning] the work they were doing for us, so that you might select evidence which you consider useful.'

It was not, by then, unexpected. Neither was it overly helpful, although following later representation Lowe would make it clear that the response of the agencies of other governments was a matter for them, and the Crown Office would not intervene. Christmas and New Year slipped by, unrecognised in the continuous round of preparation for that February date in Vilnius. Almost unrecognised . . . Peter Watson was presented by a colleague on Christmas Eve in his office with a large fur hat.

Early in January it was agreed that Len Murray should fly to Germany as a matter of urgency. A witness there named Franz Weiss had already given evidence in German hearings about the brutality of the Lithuanian battalions. Nobody knew whether or not he was prepared to speak up again, this time to a British court.

At the same time, Peter Watson called in the Mounties. The Royal Canadian Mounted Police War Crimes Section had been making its own inquiries. They were asked for the same broad span of material as had been requested of the United States, Australia, Germany, Israel, the Soviet Union – anything

and everything on the activities of that mobile unit of Lithuanian volunteers in 1941.

   And as information returned to Glasgow, it was duplica-
ted and sent out around the world, to all of the relevant
agencies, in the hope that a constant updating might provoke
a new and freshly helpful response. The office of Levy &
McRae, and Peter Watson's home, became a temporary, frantic
clearing house of war-crimes testimony. If this returned just
one witness, one atom of evidence which could swing the trial,
it would be worth while. And still, looking at the short weeks
ahead, Watson felt like a one-legged man at the foot of Everest.
He would write to Neal Sher of the American OSI in Washing-
ton on 3 January, just 11 days before the closing date for the
submission of documentation to the court: 'It would be a fair
statement that Scottish Television's position at the moment is
not an easy one and we are far from confident that Scottish
Television will succeed in their task. I would obviously ask you
to regard this letter as CONFIDENTIAL . . .'

Tomlinson had a new companion when he flew for the third
time in 12 months to Lithuania on 2 January 1992. Peter Watson
was sitting beside him. Watson considered himself to be an
experienced traveller, having holidayed extensively abroad and
been taken by his work across the Western world. He had,
however, never moved beyond the Iron Curtain, and he
anticipated a fascinating experience. 'You will not believe your
eyes,' Tomlinson had told the lawyer, who responded with
attempted dignity, impressing upon the journalist his wide
experience of the world beyond Scotland. But Tomlinson had
been right.

   They flew to Budapest, and from Budapest to East Berlin,
and from there to Vilnius. For Watson, the journey was a
collapse down ten or 20 rungs of the ladder of perceived
reality. At Budapest, the most sophisticated outpost of the
Eastern bloc, the telephone kiosks at first caught the eye: old-
fashioned, robust, mechanical apparatus. The airport had an

austere quality to it; a heavy military presence; news-stands with a mere handful of titles on display. People ate not in cafés or restaurants but out of lunch-boxes.

Templehof Airport in East Berlin had all of the characteristics of Eastern European architecture: massive, masculine communist designs owing more than a small debt to the visions of Albert Speer, and vast, gaping, high-ceilinged hallways, unheated and dimly lit. Rows of dead shops sold nothing of any interest.

A small 30-seater aeroplane took them from Templehof to Vilnius. People looked at the two Scots' clothing as if they had just stepped down from the Starship Enterprise. For them to be envious of our couture, thought Watson, indicates an unexpected degree of poverty. It was 20 degrees below zero at ground level outside, and the interior of the aircraft was freezing. As the plane took off they were presented with two slices each of smoked sausage. All of their fellow passengers ate it with enthusiasm. Watson was not yet aware that their destination, Vilnius, was suffering acutely from food shortages. He left his sausage.

There was no bar service. He got up to go to the toilet, and discovered at the back of the aeroplane a steward and stewardess partying with a bottle of vodka behind a curtain. They offered a drink to Watson. He took it gratefully. They spoke English, and he told them that he and his colleague were travelling on business. They were friendly and curious, and he was thankful for the personal contact. These were the people that he had been brought up to believe were ready to drop Soviet bombs on his country. Yet they were not frightening. On the contrary, they extended a courteous and welcoming hand of friendship.

Vilnius Airport made Templehof look like a state-of-the-art aerodrome. This is dire, thought Watson. This is desperate. Nothing looked younger than 30 years old. Guards carrying machine-guns shuffled about, suspicion clouding their features. The tension in the air was palpable, like a material thing.

The terminal was so poorly lit that Watson at first thought it to be closed. He slipped on oil on the tarmac. There was no doubting it, Tomlinson had been right.

'The Hotel Lietuva,' their driver told the two men, 'was once the finest in the whole of the Soviet Union.' On the way, Watson, peering through the window of the Lada, was aware of something commonplace which was missing from the drab streets. Something seen everywhere in the rest of the world . . . where are the advertisements? The neon signs above cafés and bars? And the city smelt, in the absence of any anti-pollution regulations, of carbon monoxide and a cocktail from hell of industrial waste.

The doors, Watson noticed, at the vestibule of the Hotel Lietuva did not match each other and did not fit their frames. Paradoxically, the reception area was a bustle of important activity, as if it were in the centre of New York or London, and yet it resembled a hostel for the homeless.

Watson telephoned reception from his room to report the fact that he had no light bulbs. There was a shortage of such goods, and consequently his had been stolen. Curiously, each room in the 21-storey hotel Lietuva was connected to reception by its own telephone line. You rang reception as if you were ringing the Lietuva from any other part of the city. His call rang out. Nobody answered, so he descended by lift to report the insufficiency of bulbs in person. He began to wonder if it was such a good idea to invite Lord Milligan to Lithuania.

Tomlinson had told Watson in Scotland that the most effective currency in this place was cigarettes, condoms and tights. Having no wish to explain to his wife why he was setting off for a week in Eastern Europe with a bulk purchase of prophylactics, Watson decided to skip over them. He bought the cigarettes, though, and a few days before leaving had made an unobtrusive visit to his local supermarket to buy 30 sets of ladies' tights. Having been advised that they liked them multi-coloured and in the large variety, he effected the transaction and left, vaguely hoping that he would not be searched at the airport.

It was worth it. A pair of ladies' tights got you a long way in Lithuania. When the light bulbs had not been replaced within two hours the lawyer turned to corruption. He meekly offered a pair of tights to his floor superintendent, pointing simultaneously at the empty light sockets. She exclaimed in amazement, pocketed the tights, and within minutes an electrician appeared. Watson had light. He slipped the electrician 20 Benson & Hedges. It was easy, when you got the hang of it. He could look Tomlinson in the eye, one old Eastern hand to another. He did not yet know, as he sat drinking duty-free whisky on a bed stained with small red insects, surrounded by his luggage, his lap-top computer and printer, that it could take up to 48 hours to connect an international telephone call and that six hours' notice was required before a fax could be transmitted from Vilnius. The small mountain that he had seen before him back in Glasgow had detached itself from the surface of the earth and was orbiting out of sight. How do you prepare a case here? How do you exist here? He felt naïve, and lost, and he longed to be practising law at home in the spoilt, degenerate comforts of Strathclyde.

'Think of the movie, wee man,' Tomlinson said to the 5' 11" Watson. 'That's what it's about. Come on, I'll show you the Black Bar.'

The barman, Jorgis, took their order for steamed chicken and boiled potatoes and poured two beers.

'Are we going to win, wee man?' asked Tomlinson, looking suddenly vulnerable. 'Will we win?'

Watson pulled himself together. This good man does not deserve this, he reminded himself. 'If we get everything, Tommo. If we get the material.'

Jorgis returned with their meals. In the days to come, the barman would make every effort to befriend the two men. Why they could not guess – they looked disparagingly upon his liquor collection and turned up their noses at his food –

until he appeared one evening with a notebook and asked for an interpretation of the Scots phrases which he had encountered while studying the collected works of Robert Burns.

They got down to the ritual task of locating witnesses and determining who could and who would testify, either in Scotland or in Lithuania, of locating documents, of discovering how far the new Lithuanian authorities would grant access to papers and information which had previously lain within the fiefdom of the KGB.

It was not easy. Vydmantis Viskaukas had permission from his Lithuanian government to co-operate, and he was aware, naturally, of the massive international interest which had been generated in the activities of the 12th Lithuanian Battalion. He knew that he was about to assist a Scottish Crown Office investigation into Antanas Gecas. He had been approached by the governments of other countries – such as Australia – with suspected Lithuanian war criminals on their territory. But Watson and Tomlinson represented no government. They were in Lithuania on behalf of a private company which was being sued for defamation, and the idea of civil litigation was somewhat foreign to Eastern Europe. They were allowed to see some papers and to dictate on-the-spot translations, but not to copy them. Watson had permanently to juggle the restrictions imposed by the Lithuanian authorities regarding what he was permitted to see and to use, with the limitations of what would be acceptable to a Scottish court. Essentially the defence required eye-witness testimony which referred to and was supplemented by documentation, working back into secondary sources and additional historical evidence.

Tomlinson took Watson to the Ninth Fort at Kaunas. In that despairing wilderness, in that building which seemed to ooze evil from every crack in its masonry, Watson saw the exhibit of an infant's pair of shoes. Already homesick and missing his two young girls, he broke down and wept. Tomlinson stood by, not diffident but not interfering. 'I cried too, when I saw those the first time,' he said finally. Outside the fort the plain was covered by an endless swarm of large black crows, all picking at the ground as if sent back by spirits to uncover the awful secrets which lay hidden in the ancient earth. Watson recited the Lord's Prayer to himself, quietly. Weeks later Watson would attend a christening at his local church. He stood there with his wife while the minister carried the infant among the congregation. The church was warm. They were happy and smiling. Then tears filled his eyes and he could hardly bear the weight of contradiction between what he was witnessing in Glasgow and what he had left behind in those stark plains spread with carrion.

They took on another translator to assist Alan Henderson, another former Intourist employee named Zeta Makutiena, a woman who turned out to have a thoroughly un-Lithuanian dedication to hard work, meeting deadlines, and achieving efficiency, but it quickly became obvious to Watson that he could not accomplish all that needed doing in one visit. Even the supposedly simple task of obtaining a birth certificate to confirm somebody's age proved a monumental task. Zeta Makutiena, armed with dollar bills and with an impromptu letterhead printed up on Watson's laptop, did her best to buy and bluff her way through red tape, but even she could not combat what the Scots came to know as 'Lithuanian slippage': the self-conscious, almost delighted ability of the locals to break appointments, discover obstacles and impede the smooth flow of any investigation. 'Lithuanian slippage', thought Watson, explains why a country which produces more food than it eats, nonetheless suffers from acute food shortages. And behind all of their work, hanging sullenly over their contacts with most Lithuanians, was the country's strong, residual streak of anti-semitism. Did not the Jews ask for it? Why don't you hear the other side of the story? Anti-semitic graffiti was appearing on the walls: 'What The German's Didn't Finish, We Will'. Spoken, half-spoken, or just there, indeterminately in the background, this terrible contemporary reminder of how holocausts gain ground and win the hearts

and minds of Gentiles informed much of Peter Watson's first
few days in Lithuania. He trawled through documents for a
week, and returned to Glasgow, making arrangements for
another trip back to Lithuania.

In Scotland he found Len Murray, returned from
Germany with a report on a meeting with the former German
soldier Franz Weiss, who had served with the forces of the
Reich in Byelorussia in 1941. Weiss would not travel to give
evidence, read Murray's report. 'He has had to live with
this affair for the past 50 years. He has continually been
asked questions about it for the past 30-odd years. He is
praying for the day when he will be asked questions about
it for the last time. Even now he still cannot come to terms
with it.'

But Weiss remembered the 'aktions'. The shooting, he
said, was all done by Lithuanians. 'Gecas,' Murray had suggested to him, 'said that the Lithuanians acted as guards and
the Germans went in and exterminated the Jews.'

'That is a lie,' said Weiss. 'Gecas must know it is a lie, and
what Gecas has done is to reverse precisely what happened.'
Weiss and his German colleagues rounded up the Jews, he
said, and handed them over to the Lithuanians. The Germans
then walked the streets to ensure that nobody got in or out
while this aktion was going on. 'The Lithuanians took the Jews
away and shot them.'

Slowly the evidence was coming in. Translated papers
from the former Soviet Union, witness statements from Lithuania, court transcripts of the trials of war criminals from the
files of the KGB were being augmented by material produced
by attorneys which Levy & McRae had instructed in Germany
and in the USA. Circumstantial evidence alone would never
beat Antanas Gecas in court, but the circumstances which
surrounded his battalion's presence in Lithuania and Byelorussia in 1941 had to be established . . . and they were,
gradually, being established beyond dispute.

And then they achieved a major breakthrough. Professor

Raul Hilberg, the internationally acknowledged supreme expert on the subject of the holocaust and author of the masterwork on the subject, *The Destruction of the European Jews*, agreed to work with the defence as an adviser and to appear as a witness. This hugely important historian was already committed to give evidence at other war-crimes trials in different parts of the world, but he put himself at Scottish Television's disposal for the duration of their courtroom struggle with Antanas Gecas.

Watson ploughed on, pushing, berating, encouraging his colleagues, his staff, and the defenders who had employed him. Results were beginning to show. The pile of papers which were due to be filed as evidence by 14 January was a yard high and growing. Things were falling into place. Witnesses were gathering.

The lawyer's cautious, grudging, but mutually respectful relationship with the new Lithuanian procurator, Vydmantis Viskaukas, would prove to be important. At the end of Watson's and Tomlinson's first trip to Lithuania they had dined Viskaukas at the Black Bar, and he had stood to offer toasts. Addressing Watson, he had said that the Scot could have made a good lawyer even in Lithuania. After a moment's thought, Watson chose to take it as a compliment, although his notion of being a successful lawyer did not include occupying two unheated rooms on the 15th floor of a Vilnius tower block.

Viskaukas had not, unlike his predecessors in Soviet-controlled Lithuania, been KGB, but he was nonetheless anxious not to embarrass former colleagues who had worked in the old system. Under pressure he had agreed to deliver a summary of the KGB archives dealing with the activities of Lithuanians during the Nazi occupation. Watson became the first non-Soviet citizen to see these papers, which he and Tomlinson would christen the 'Crown Jewels'. Not even the Crown Office had gained access to these papers, which revealed a previously uncovered depth of information relating to Antanas Gecevicius. The summary was not evidence, but it made clear what damning evidence was available, who the witnesses might be, what documents existed – not only Soviet documents, but also captured German papers – proof positive of the behaviour of the 12th Battalion. It was an enormous find. It provided a game-plan for the defence. All they had to do was slot admissible evidence into the framework offered by the Crown Jewels. That was all . . .

Witnesses were vital. The defence could not rely on what a Scottish court would regard as secondary evidence – a category which included statements that witnesses had given in earlier years, to the KGB, or to Lithuanian procurators, or in a Soviet war-crimes trial. If witnesses were still alive, they had either to be persuaded to take the stand, or they had to be interviewed afresh under the strictures of Scottish law. Many were not alive. Some had died of old age. Some had been executed for their crimes. And some of the remainder were like Mickevicius, fed up with questions, or pressured from other sources, and prepared at best to remain silent and at worst to recant previous confessions.

So the search for available old men with tales to tell, who were still willing to tell them, went on day and night as the last days passed before the commencement of the trial. Names were thrown up from every direction, followed by frantic efforts to discover if they were dead or alive and, if the latter, could stand upright and talk and, if they could – where did they live? Where, on those shattered, dispossessed plains had they finally settled, after the maelstrom of the Great Patriotic War had swept over their homelands, after they themselves had returned from a decade or two in the Gulag Archipelago?

Watson returned to Lithuania with Tomlinson to take more affidavits. Leonas Mickevicius was, once again, uncooperative. He would not at first allow Watson and Henderson into his house. Watson persisted. After hedging and equivocating, he was shown by Peter Watson the transcript of his filmed interview in *Crimes of War*. 'I deny that I was filmed,' he said. 'Scottish Television arrived here with questions written out to be answered yes or no. I think the interpreter must work for the KGB. I am told that I agreed that the protocols were correct in January 1991, when I was interviewed by someone called Leonard George Murray. I think he is a member of the KGB.'

'Bob Tomlinson of Scottish Television,' said Watson, 'is outside in a car. Shall we bring him up so that you can tell him this?'

'You must all leave,' said Mickevicius. 'Now. I do not wish to be involved.'

'This witness was extremely difficult,' wrote Watson later in a footnote to the affidavit. It was a body blow. Not only would Mickevicius now be less than useless to the defence, he was potentially a witness for Antanas Gecas.

Over in Alytus, Juozas Aleksynas held true. In a calm, matter-of-fact way, he assured Watson that while 'I am getting a bit fed up repeating it', everything that he had said, to the Scottish Television cameras, to Murray, to his local procurators, had been true. And . . . 'I will attend the Scottish Court in Vilnius. I am anxious, however, that I am taken and brought back each day, since I have to look after my pigs and my grandchildren.'

That can be arranged, thought Watson in a wave of relief. It was difficult not to like Aleksynas. Who was he? Was he a monster who had put women and children to death? Or was he the caring grandfather struggling in his old age to look after his dead son's children? He was both, of course. Terribly, those deeds could obviously be accommodated within one human being in the short span of one life. Ordinary men; they were all ordinary men. Watson and Tomlinson too were ordinary men. Who on earth could explain the capacity for good and evil, kindness and brutality, in ordinary men? Watson chatted with Aleksynas about young children and the trials involved in their upbringing, about Scotland and about Lithuania.

Watson had been told by Murray and Tomlinson that the third of those ordinary men, Motiejus Migonis, was a good witness. So he appeared, when Watson visited the old man. 'All of what I have said . . . is accurate,' Migonis affirmed. 'I cannot add to it nor would I seek to withdraw from it. It is the truth and it has always been my evidence, and it will be my evidence before the Scottish court.'

Migonis, Watson noted to his counsel, 'is an impressive witness who will not be moved from his account'. Four weeks later he would have anguished cause to regret that footnote.

The lawyer moved on by Lada, with a driver who had never before driven outside Vilnius, to the country home of one of the 'new' witnesses, a 75-year-old former labourer named Leonas Pocevicius. En route the car broke down, and in −15° the driver stripped down the carburettor. 'Just remember, wee man,' said Tomlinson to Watson, 'I was on the last helicopter out when the Americans left Saigon. Just think of all the stories you'll be able to tell.'

Pocevicius's memory of the place names of different sites of atrocities that he had witnessed while a member of the 12th Battalion was blurred: there had been so many of them, in such a short period of time.

But he remembered Minsk. He remembered there the hanging of 'five or six people, including one woman. They were placed on the back of a lorry with the nooses round their neck and the rope attached to poles, and then the lorry was taken away and they were left to swing on the rope and hang to death.'

And on they went through the lucky-dip barrel of names, to Edvardas Goga, Juozas Grigonis, to some who would and some who would not testify, to those who would travel to Vilnius and to those who would even travel to Edinburgh, through good and bad statements, praying all along that these old men would repeat in court the damning evidence which they calmly gave in private.

They got to the house of one Leonas Stonkus and asked

for the former soldier. 'He's dead,' said the man answering the door.

Watson turned away. Three weeks earlier he would have left without second thought. But this was a society brought up among informers, under the KGB, in a climate of mistrust and fear. He stopped and looked at Tomlinson. 'How dead do you think he is?' He looked round, and across the road he could see a neighbour working beneath the bonnet of another broken Lada. The two men and their interpreter walked over. Watson took out a ten-dollar bill and ripped it in two. He gave one half to the neighbour.

'Tell him,' he told the interpreter, 'that we need to speak to Leonas Stonkus. If he will lead us to him, I will give him the other half.'

The neighbour slammed down his bonnet, got into his car and started the engine. They followed him through the snow, out of the village and along a winding road through thick forest. They arrived eventually at a small cottage tucked among trees. They entered. A woman and children were in the wooden building, with a man of about 70. Tomlinson led the children away. Watson could hear him in the background, giving them sweets and laughing.

'Are you Leonas Stonkus?' he asked the old man.

'Yes.'

'I wish to ask you about a man called Antanas Gecevicius.'

Stonkus had been with Gecevicius and the 12th Battalion until the end, in the Lithuanian town of Taurage in 1944, when the retreating Germans advised them to go to Italy to renew their struggle against the Allies there.

'We were lined up in Taurage and Gecevicius – I can't say whether his own words or whether he was translating for a German officer – said that it was stupid to seek repatriation in Lithuania because we would be skinned alive for the crimes committed in Byelorussia. He was trying persuade us to go to Italy.'

One by one, the new pieces fell into place.

Edvardas Goga was, they had been told, a politician in the new Lithuania. Would he want to discuss his past? Goga was clearly anxious to impress upon his visitors that he was something of a man apart, more than the ordinary Lithuanian. He recalled a Byelorussian town, one of many, into which the 12th Battalion had marched late in 1941 . . .

'We were to search every single home in the town looking for Jews. It was only Jews we were to look for. We were to examine their papers and all the Jews were to be identified and to be taken to the town square . . . Women, children, the old, the young, everyone . . . It was awful. The Germans then stood and discussed where the killing was to take place and it was decided it would take place in what you might describe as a quarry for sand.

'There were holes there from the quarrying and the Jews were herded in groups and shot. The Germans and ourselves took part . . . The other incident which I can recall was a much bigger incident and most certainly did involve Gecevicius. [It] involved the death of at least 10,000 prisoners-of-war. The shooting took place over three days or more . . . It was in the Minsk area . . . the prisoners-of-war were marched between the two rows of soldiers. This was to stop anyone escaping. They were marched for, say, half a kilometre or perhaps a kilometre from the prisoner-of-war camp. The pits had already been dug. They were 40 metres in length, I would say, two metres deep and perhaps three metres wide. The prisoners were taken in order to be shot . . . 100 at a time, perhaps. This went on for three days or so . . .

'The shooting at the pits,' continued Edvardas Goga, 'was done by members of the 12th Lithuanian Battalion. There is no doubt it was our battalion. Virtually the whole battalion was involved . . .'

Such activities were not only against the Geneva Convention; they also counted as crimes of war. Goga, to Watson's great relief, agreed to travel and repeat his testimony in Edinburgh, before a Scottish court.

The simplest administrative tasks assumed, in Lithuania, epic proportions. There was not a paper clip or a rubber band to be found. There was hardly a single working typewriter. Vydmantis Viskaukas had such a machine. Its single ribbon was five years old. Everything for the hearing of the commission – the part of the trial to be conducted in Lithuania – would have to be imported, from recording equipment down to Lord Milligan's toilet paper.

Then Watson heard that the judge's charming wife had decided to accompany her husband. What to do with Lady Milligan? How to insulate her from the rigours of Lithuanian life? The defence met with the British ambassador, Michael Peart, who, despite the fact that his new embassy offices possessed little more than a couch and two chairs, offered his full assistance – so much so that Tomlinson felt obliged to do something to indicate Scottish Television's corporate thanks to Peart.

A small bombshell was exploded just a few days before the hearing in Vilnius was due to start. A letter had been delivered to some of the main Lithuanian witnesses, including Aleksynas and Migonis, explaining to them that if in the course of their evidence to the Scottish court they admitted to crimes for which they had not already been tried and sentenced in the former Soviet republic of Lithuania, they may be subject to procedures in the new Lithuania. To men in their late 70s, it was an unappetising prospect. Watson could find no explanation for these letters. A local representative of the Weisenthal Centre mentioned to him that the father of the Lithuanian chief justice, Judge Losys, had worked in the Ninth Fort at Kaunas during the Second World War. Draw your own conclusions, the woman said.

There was no means of forcing these Lithuanian witnesses to turn up in court, in Lithuania or in Scotland. There was no effective subpoena available to Peter Watson. He simply had to cajole and reassure. Leonas Pocevicius insisted that he had been reliably informed that, as a result of his testimony,

Antanas Gecevicius would be hanged in Great Britain. Watson
drew a deep breath and set about explaining to the Lithuanian
firstly the concept of a society which did not have the death
penalty, and then the principles of civil law. Then he removed
Pocevicius from his shed in the country and accommodated
him in a safe house in Vilnius. Many Lithuanians other than
the expatriate Antanas Gecas were interested, it was apparent,
in seeing this commissioned hearing in Vilnius derailed. There
was an understandable anxiety in the newly liberated Lithuania that the country should not achieve a fresh notoriety in
the media of the Western world as a source of war criminals.
One night after arriving in Vilnius, Graham Fordyce answered
a knock on his room door. Two men forced their way in, beat
him up, and escaped. The defence team pragmatically decided
to write the incident off as a common assault in search of
foreign currency. But nobody really knew. Watson and Tomlinson grew convinced that they were being followed and that
their telephones were bugged.

Rooms were rented for the party of Westerners who
would travel with the commission, and the one acceptable
restaurant in Vilnius was put on standby. Cars were hired. An
old, beat-up BMW was uncovered for 'Lordus Milligan', as the
interpreter Zeta described his eminence. It was produced with
great pride from amid a sea of Ladas. David Scott arrived to
inspect his troops.

And suddenly it dawned on Watson, as he was pondering
the prospect of exporting a handful of Lithuanians to Scotland
to give evidence there: none of them had a passport. There
was not a Lithuanian passport for them to possess. The old
Soviet passports, even had they owned one – which, of course,
they did not – were as useless as a rouble piece outside the
Soviet border. Lithuanian passports had been ordered by the
new government from a British printer; but they had been
returned because of a spelling mistake. Watson appealed to
Ambassador Peart for help. It worked. The witness Edvardas
Goga, in fact, would receive the first Lithuanian passport and

visa to be issued to enable a Lithuanian citizen to travel to the United Kingdom.

Time had fled. January was gone. Sooner than anybody would have wished, a Scottish typist spelled out on legal manuscript the words: 'At Vilnius, Lithuania, on Tuesday, the eleventh day of February, nineteen hundred and ninety-two years, there was presented to Lord Milligan, Certified Copies of Interlocutors pronounced by him in an Action in which ANTONY GECAS, formerly known as ANTANAS GECEVI-CIUS, residing at 3 Moston Terrace, Edinburgh, is Pursuer, and SCOTTISH TELEVISION plc . . . are defenders.'

The proof was on.

12

Juozas Janos Aleksynas was the first witness to the first
Scottish court ever to conduct a hearing outside Great Britain.
Clothed in a clean old suit, the wry, composed 78-year-old
took the stand to receive the opening friendly questions of
Colin Campbell QC.

He had joined the 12th Battalion early in its life, in July
1941, when it was still the 2nd Battalion, Aleksynas said. 'I was
secretary of the trade union during the Soviet period, and then
after the German occupation people like secretaries of the trade
unions were persecuted, and I just first went to live with my
sister, trying to avoid persecution, and later I joined this
battalion.' Before they left Lithuania in the autumn of 1941, he
said, sub-lieutenant Antanas Gecevicius had become his unit
commander. As a former officer in the Lithuanian airforce,
Gecevicius wore a navy-blue uniform. The rest of the battalion
were in green.

Aleksynas told the steady stories of mass murder. Jewish
men, women and children were led to the Byelorussian pits
and shot.

'Who was it that shot the Jews in the pit?' pressed
Campbell.

'The soldiers.'

'Lithuanian soldiers.'

'Yes, Lithuanian.'

And after the shootings, officers would step forward to inspect the mass graves, said Aleksynas.

'Did Lithuanian officers ever go to check?'

'They would be among them, so they were usually standing together, and so they were to go together.'

'On this occasion did Gecevicius go with them at the time of the checking?'

'Yes, he went with them.'

'And what happened if they found any survivors?'

'Obviously they would finish him off.'

Aleksynas took the court, suspecting and unsuspecting, from Slutsk, to Minsk, to tiny, nameless villages where a small school-full of citizens were executed, to ambushes by partisans in birch groves. All that he had said before, on camera and to procurators and to courtrooms, he said, was the truth.

The court adjourned for lunch. Antanas Gecas's attorneys went off to communicate by telephone with their client's solicitors – such calls would be necessary at regular intervals throughout the hearings in Lithuania for Messrs Simpson and Armstrong, Gecas himself having taken the precaution of not travelling back to his country of birth – and Peter Watson went to the side of Aleksynas. The old man promptly offered him half of his lunch of dried meat, cheese and bread. Watson nodded a sincere, wondering gratitude, and took the food.

John Simpson lost no time when the court reconvened in establishing that Aleksynas had not actually seen Antanas Gecevicius 'finishing people off'. Aleksynas concurred comfortably. 'I haven't seen it. There was only an order to act.'

And John Simpson extracted from Juozas Aleksynas the uncomfortable details of his post-war prosecution by the returning Soviets. 'There is a difference between being charged and what you were found guilty of: do you appreciate that?'

Aleksynas certainly did. 'They just sentenced me under Section 58. If you said that, for example, Germans had better military equipment, they would give you ten years of jail.'

Did the name of Antanas Gecevicius arise during his 'trial' by the Soviets?

During interrogation, said Aleksynas.

'Was there a degree of force used in making you say these things?'

'Only the Russians, the KGB, when they interrogated me . . . It went so far as that I had to say, "Just write what you want and I am going to sign it."'

That had been immediately after the war, in 1945. Aleksynas had been imprisoned by the Red Army in the winter of 1944, when it returned to Lithuania. John Simpson had a marvellous opportunity to play one brutal totalitarian state off against another for the affection and trust of the court, and he did not miss it.

'We were taken,' said Aleksynas, '[by the Soviets in 1944/ 45] from prison into the city garden in Marijampole, the distance was about three kilometres. So we were taken from those prison cells for the interrogation of the KGB. They would cut off the buttons from your pants when you had to cross the city, and so on your way you had to hold your pants, keep them from falling down: so they knew how to make a man feel. If you thought about trying to run you wouldn't be able to do that because then your hands would come free and your pants would drop.'

Was Aleksynas still frightened of the KGB when they later questioned him?

He shrugged. 'They just treated me as a witness. I was a free man then.'

And Aleksynas's account of what had happened at Slutsk was wrong, argued John Simpson. 'I have to put it to you that the German 11th Battalion ran amok in Slutsk in these two days . . . And similarly I have to put it to you that your evidence about Mr Gecas, Mr Gecevicius, as being platoon leader and being involved in these other incidents is also wrong?'

Aleksynas rallied. 'So then,' he countered, 'I just want to

ask, if Gecevicius did not take part in all these operations, the question, does that mean that Gecevicius did not take part in any of these operations?'

'Yes,' said Simpson.

'So you mean,' continued Aleksynas, 'that Gecevicius did not take part in that battalion?'

'I,' said John Simpson, 'am supposed to be asking the questions.'

The lawyer readjusted his line of examination and closed for the kill. 'Specifically,' he said, 'I put it to you that Mr Gecas did not give any orders to shoot at the gravel pits?'

'I don't know who knows more,' replied the Lithuanian peasant caustically, 'I myself or the person who is asking me.'

'I also have to put it to you that Mr Gecevicius was not at the Soviet prisoner-of-war camp?'

'Do you mean the camp from which we were taken to dig pits?'

'Yes.'

'If he was not at the prisoner camp then he was transporting the Jews to that area.'

'Well, I put it to you that he wasn't there at all?'

'Then there is nothing to talk about.'

'I put it to you also that Mr Gecas was not present at the birch grove?'

'Then we can say,' said Aleksynas, 'that he was not in the battalion at all.'

And finally, said John Simpson, 'He was not present when Jews were being marched from the Minsk ghetto?'

'Then Gecevicius,' sighed Aleksynas, 'was nowhere at all.'

Advocate Simpson had got small change from Aleksynas. 'Lastly,' he concluded, 'I have to put it to you that Mr Gecevicius was not present at any incident where Jews were shot?'

Juozas Aleksynas had his own cynical, quizzical answer to that. 'He didn't take part,' he said, 'because he is being protected, defended for money.' That is legal reality, the old man was saying, whatever you can get people to believe, whatever legal representation you can afford. In his own case, the case of a footsoldier in the holocaust, he had had no defence and he had paid the price. The truth was, nonetheless, a different and purer thing. Would it out, in this curious setting?

The 'impressive witness' Motiejus Migonis was called next by the defence. Unwell and running a temperature, Migonis nonetheless started consistently under questioning by Richard Keen. He described how the 12th Battalion had been issued with 'Russian trophy guns' – captured weapons – in Minsk.

And then, to the consternation of the defence, Migonis began to go off the rails. At Slutsk, he said, he could not remember much of what had happened by the pits. He could not remember his orders there. He could not see what happened.

'Were people taken to the pits?' asked Richard Keen.

'They could be and they could not be. I could not prove it.'

'You know that people were taken to the pits, do you not?'

'How could I know? I didn't know such an order, because I didn't go and examine the documents where this was said.'

'I am not talking about documents, I wish to ask you what you saw.'

'If I didn't see anything,' stonewalled Migonis, 'how can I say that I did?'

Keen quickly covered his tracks by getting Migonis to accept that he had signed his previous statements to Len Murray and Peter Watson, but some damage was undeniably done. And Migonis had still to face John Simpson.

Simpson wasted no time. 'Did you ever take part in executions at pits near Kaunas or Minsk?'

'I didn't happen to do that,' replied Migonis.

'Did you ever at any time see Mr Gecevicius himself shoot people at the pits with a pistol?'

'No.'

John Simpson then took Motiejus Migonis back to 1987, when he had cheerfully agreed to revisit, with the Scottish Television cameras, the site of the massacre at Slutsk.

'Do you remember in 1987 being taken by some people in Scotland to a wood?'

'Yes, I was there myself.'

'Had you ever been in that wood yourself before?'

'No,' replied Migonis, 'I haven't. Why should I walk in that wood?'

'But have you ever been there before?'

'I can't really say because I don't quite recollect it.'

John Simpson ended his satisfactory examination. The course of the prosecution was clear. By emphasising the corrupt tyranny over the people of Lithuania of the Soviet Union, they would attempt to discredit all previous testimony, written or spoken, as unreliably coerced by the KGB. John Simpson's witness in Vilnius would add weight to that line.

Father Alfonsas Svarinskas was a 68-year-old Lithuanian priest; a committed nationalist who had served 22 years in Soviet prisons and who was, by 1992, a deputy in the Supreme Council of the Lithuanian Republic. He had last been released from prison in 1988, on the request to Gorbavchev of Ronald Reagan.

Father Svarinskas told the commission that under questioning by the KGB a prisoner was likely to confess to anything. He accepted, under questioning by Colin Campbell, that Jews had been murdered in Lithuania during the war – 'But there was no longer a Lithuanian republic at that time.'

The hearing in Lithuania ended. It had cost Scottish Television a great deal of money, and it had been far from an unqualified success for the defence. The court moved back to Edinburgh.

In the austere surroundings of the High Court, Edvardas Goga told his story of the massacre in Byelorussia of 10,000 prisoners-of-war.

'Was Gecevicius at this operation?' Colin Campbell asked the Lithuanian politician.

'Yes, he was there.'

'Can you describe him physically to us?'

'I am not an artist.'

'Was he short, a tall man?'

'Yes, he was tall, sportslike figure, beautifully built, perhaps just about six feet tall. He perhaps would stand apart among the other soldiers because he was tall.'

The Queen's Counsel Donald Robertson had joined Antanas Gecas's legal team for its travails in Scotland.

'The purpose of being sent [to the Minsk area],' he suggested to Goga, 'was to do what you had joined the battalion to do, to fight against Bolshevism?'

'Yes, that is right. We did not expect further things: we thought we would just be serving for keeping public order, the internal order of the country . . . our impression was that every Soviet was a murderer.'

'It was suggested to you this morning that you remember Lieutenant Gecevicius being there: is the fact of the matter that you don't remember whether he was there or not?'

'How so? I have said quite precisely.'

'After the persons were shot,' asked Donald Robertson, 'and fell into the pits – were they shot in the pits or were they shot standing beside the pits?'

'They were shot in the pits. We saw at a distance that they were stripped at the pits, then they were finished off there.'

'Shot by soldiers?'

'They were shot both by soldiers and officers, German and Lithuanian.'

'At the same time?'

'Yes, at the same time.'

'Were you able to see from where you were standing

whether every officer shot, fired his gun, fired his pistol, or
only some of them?'

'I wouldn't be able to say precisely that everyone was
shooting.'

Donald Robertson concluded his work with Edvardas
Goga by sympathetic questioning on the nature of Soviet
interrogation, and by commenting that Mr Goga may be having
trouble in distinguishing between the names of two Lithuanian
army officers. One, to whom he had referred, was called
Gecauskis. The other was Gecevicius.

And then, Robert Kennedy Tomlinson was called to give
evidence. Richard Keen ran Tomlinson through his involvement in the Antanas Gecas affair, from the clipping from the
Daily Record in 1986. Early in his researches, the journalist told
the court, after receipt of Neal Sher's interview with Gecas, 'I
actually thought that in terms of alleged war crimes, that we
were simply looking at the murder of 150 people at that point.
I didn't realise what we were about to find in later months.'

Tomlinson went over the old, rehearsed ground: the
discovery of the Ratline, the making of *Britain, The Nazi
Safehouse*, the opening of the Pandora's box which had led him
– fatefully, inevitably, it seemed now – to this witness stand.
He told of Professor Gerald Draper and of Eli Rosenbaum.
How long ago it seemed. Half a decade out of his life. He
related the stories of the first visits to the Soviet Union, with
and without a television crew. He described the trip to Slutsk
with Motiejus Migonis . . .

'Who requested the presence of Mr Migonis on the visit
to Slutsk?' interspersed Richard Keen.

'Ross Wilson, our director, decided that it looked as if the
film was all going to be what is known in our profession as
"talking heads", people just sitting down or standing . . . So
we invited Mr Migonis, we did a formal interview in his house
with him, but we asked him if he was willing, would he come
to Slutsk to the site of the massacre, and he said: "Of course I
am willing".'

Donald Robertson stepped forward. Drawing a picture of Antanas Gecas as a peacefully retired citizen harassed and misrepresented by the media, he suggested to Tomlinson that even the first interview had been later misused by Scottish Television – 'Did you not tell him what you were going to do with it?'

'I didn't tell him.'

'Why not?'

'Because I didn't know what we were going to do with it . . . I told him I wanted to interview him about the allegations. We filmed the interview. It subsequently turned out that given the information that arrived from the United States that quite clearly the interview was of greater value than as a news story, therefore part of it was incorporated into the film *Britain, The Nazi Safehouse.*'

Eli Rosenbaum had been taken along to the house of Antanas Gecas almost mischievously, implied Donald Robertson's line of questioning – 'It was obvious to you that Mr Rosenbaum was coming along in your company wanting to get some information with a view to investigating Mr Gecas, with a possibility of having him prosecuted.'

No, replied Tomlinson. 'It would have been of great value to us if someone who had very detailed information on the massacre at Slutsk, the massacre at Minsk, and the activities of the 12th Battalion, namely someone from OSI – it would have been of great value to us as film-makers to have had that person put questions [to Gecas] rather than myself.' Tomlinson also denied that Rosenbaum had been taken to Moston Terrace to be filmed having the door slammed in his face. 'It is very expensive to film a door being shut on you.'

Robertson came to his point. Tomlinson was a man driven beyond the point of reason. 'Would it be true to say that you were angered that there was a Nazi war criminal living in Scotland and that you were determined to do whatever you could to force the British government to take action?'

'It is not true to say,' replied Tomlinson, 'that I was

determined to do anything I could to make the British government take action. What I did feel, as many of our viewers did
feel, and many readers and newspapers felt, was a sense of
shock that this was a British policy, and that our job as
journalists is surely to highlight problems.'

Was Tomlinson aware that the Soviet courts which Gecas
would have faced had he been extradited, were radically
different to Scottish courts? 'I have never been a court
reporter,' he said. Aside from a speeding offence in 1966, this
was his first time spent inside a courtroom.

'It didn't occur to you,' continued the QC relentlessly,
'and I take it you were not told, that what the Soviets really
might be interested in was having these people put on trial in
Russia for treason, for fighting against the Motherland . . . It
never occurred to you that they might want to blacken the
name of Lithuanian nationalists, people who might have had
aspirations for the independence of these countries?'

'I was not interested in what people's whims, fancies,
desires or aspirations were,' said Tomlinson. 'I was interested
in the fact that it was alleged there were 17, and I now
discovered 51, alleged war criminals living in Britain.'

This Soviet disinformation campaign, suggested Donald
Robertson, had used Bob Tomlinson so cleverly that it had
been able to get him to publicise the site of the Nazi atrocities
at Hatyn, in order to draw a smokescreen over the Russian
atrocities at the Forest of Hatyn – an entirely different place.
Had Tomlinson not thought it peculiar that state procurators
set up his interviews with witnesses in Lithuania, that Bacucionis and Kolesnikova escorted them to the interviewees,
and were even present while the cameras were rolling? He
had been at best naïve, was Robertson's point: 'You went
on the basis that they were all honourable, honest, independent, straightforward persons who had no connection
with the KGB, and the procurator was just like the procurator fiscal in Scotland, and you could just take what they told
you.'

Even the evidence of Migonis, filmed live in the woods outside Slutsk, had been discredited by his own admission at the hearing in Vilnius that he did not 'quite recollect' having been there before, at any time, argued Donald Robertson.

'And would you have put him in the programme at all if he had said . . . that he was fighting against the Russians and against communism, for freedom, that he never took part in executions at pits in Kaunas or Minsk and that he had never seen Mr Gecevicius shoot persons at pits?'

'Had there been any doubt in our minds whatsoever he had not witnessed the mass murder of Jews at various places, if there was any doubt in our minds that he did not know Gecevicius, had there been any doubt in our minds that he saw Gecevicius murder people, he would not have been included in the programme.'

Raul Hilberg, the 65-year-old Emeritus Professor of Political Science at the University of Vermont and the greatest living authority on the subject of the holocaust, next took the witness stand. He would be there for three days, offering information on the destruction of the European Jews. The defence had given up on their plans to present many more witnesses from the Soviet Union or from Lithuania to the court: it was too dangerous; they would be portrayed as KGB or as unsafe witnesses, corrupted by the old Soviet system. It would be difficult, however, for anybody to depict Professor Hilberg as an unsafe witness. There was no better person to bring the jigsaw close to completion.

During and after the Soviet occupation of Lithuania in 1940, Professor Hilberg was asked by Colin Campbell, 'was there an identification of the Jewish citizens in Lithuania with the communist occupiers?'

'I do believe a number of Lithuanians made that identification,' he replied, 'owing to the fact that there was in the Soviet Secret Police any number – how many I couldn't tell you – of persons who were of Jewish origin. I believe that

these individuals in particular were considered a dispropor-
tionate number.'

'Were all Jews sympathetic to the communist occupiers?'

'No, I would say that was a minority. Generally one may
make the statement, that for perhaps all of Europe the Jews
were sympathetic to the communist movement as a messianic,
idealistic matter in somewhat larger proportions than non-
Jews; that is to say that if one percent of the non-Jewish
population identified with communism, among the Jews it
might be two or three percent. It was not, however, a very
large number.'

The so-called 'final solution', said Hilberg, had two stages:
'Stage one applied to the territory occupied from the Soviet
Union, and stage two applied to the rest of Europe. In any
case, the two methods were radically different, because in the
case of the Soviet Union the killers were going to come to the
victims, whereas in the rest of Europe the victims were going
to be shipped to the killers.'

Stage one was officially underway by mid-August 1941,
'especially in the East, where Heinrich Himmler, for example,
on or about 15 August literally climbed aboard a truck and,
speaking to the high-ranking SS men, announced it was the
policy of Adolf Hitler to annihilate the Jews. He did this in the
occupied city of Minsk . . . It took a little longer, I believe, for
the idea to sink in in other more Western territories, but there
was no question that the decision as such had been made by
the end of the summer of 1941, covering all of Europe, covering
the physical annihilation of men, women and children who
were defined as Jewish.'

Raul Hilberg took the court carefully through the meticu-
lous German preparations for that annihilation: their graded
system of policing in their newly won territories, and the
establishment of volunteer local police battalions, recruited
chiefly from among the armed forces of the occupied eastlands.
'It was the German wish,' he said, 'that the partisans be
disbanded and that five reliable companies be formed [in

Lithuania]. By reliable, the Germans meant . . . people who
would be willing to subjugate themselves to a military type of
discipline . . . They wanted, in short, a company that was
more like what they would recognise in a German police
company . . . And two of the companies were appropriated by
the Einsatzgruppen, one of them to shoot Jews, that is on an
ongoing, day by day basis.'

'Would it be necessary,' Colin Campbell asked him, 'for
the Germans to have somebody in the Lithuanian Auxiliary
Battalion who understood the orders the Germans were
giving?'

'Absolutely. Particularly so in the case of officers. It would
have been inconceivable actually to appoint officers in these
units who would not have a command of the German
language.'

Painstakingly Professor Hilberg dissected the captured
Nazi papers which revealed the movements, command structure, actions and personnel of the 2nd/12th Lithuanian Battalion. As morning drew into afternoon and one day led on to
the next, the expert led the court like a teacher of children
through the maze of documents, from Lithuania to the fatal
fields of Slutsk. Why was it done? How did it happen? The
professor struggled for an answer . . .

'This is harder to understand,' he said. 'During our
weekend recess I went to your wonderful Modern Art Museum
and there saw Goya's etchings of the war in Spain where the
Frenchmen were engaged in some atrocities, and Goya had
written under one of these etchings "One cannot understand
why, one cannot tell why."

'This applies in a deeper sense to Byelorussia, because the
German police and the German army did not wish to commit
Napoleonic atrocities – it was, after all, a cultured nation – and
if harsh actions were necessary against defenceless men,
women and children the task was wherever possible trans-
ferred to indigenous helpers, not only the Lithuanians but also
Latvians, Ukrainians and Estonians.' The orders given to the

troops who entered Slutsk in October 1941 were, said Hilberg, unequivocal.

'Is there any suggestion,' asked Colin Campbell, 'in the historical record that members of the Lithuanian Battalion went to Slutsk to fight?'

'No.'

At Slutsk, said Professor Hilberg, 'the brutality, the sadism was assigned entirely to Lithuanians, and there was a theory that . . . an ancient hatred of Lithuanians and Jews [was] enacted here in Slutsk.'

Not all Lithuanians, of course, were involved in or supportive of those genocidal acts. A leaflet was produced during Raul Hilberg's testimony, which had been distributed by their countrymen to Lithuanian nationalists who were fighting with the Germans. It called upon them to end their murder of the Jewish population. 'The Germans began to murder the Jewish members of the people through your hands,' it read in part. 'They robbed the Jewish property. Be assured, partisan, that you will suffer the same fate. You are the tool of the German crusader for the murder of innocent inhabitants. At some point we must all say: enough of this shedding of innocent blood. Today we must proclaim an all-for-one-and-one-for-all battle against the crusader.'

Finally, asked Colin Campbell of Raul Hilberg on the morning of the professor's third day of testimony, 'If it was suggested that one particular platoon within the 1st Company, let's say for example Gecevicius's platoon, was not involved in shooting Jews . . . what comments if any would you have to that?'

'Such a suggestion is beyond credibility . . . [and] it is inconceivable to me that a platoon leader would be excused or would be absent from the scene unless he were hospitalised for a lengthy period of time due to some illness. We can reject that possibility because we have seen a document listing people who were on the sick list, and that list did not include any officers of the Lithuanian Battalion. The inescapable conclusion, therefore, is that a platoon leader was present and in action.'

'And by "action" there, we include action involving the shooting of Jewish families?'

'Yes.'

Raul Hilberg was going to be an awkward witness for Donald Robertson to question on behalf of Antanas Gecas. The QC nonetheless approached his task with gusto.

'In your view,' he suggested to Hilberg, 'the whole business of the Germans suggesting, indeed recording, actions against partisans and the trouble that they were having with partisans, is really all a façade, just an excuse for killing innocent civilians when there really wasn't any material partisan activity which worried them at all.'

This lay at the hub of Antanas Gecas's defence against allegations that he had committed war crimes. Was his battalion truly engaged in a struggle against remnants of the Red Army in Lithuania and Byelorussia, taking occasional time out to act as reluctant guards while the Germans culled some of the Jewish population? Were those apparently damning figures of 5,000 dead here, 10,000 dead there, to be found wherever Gecevicius's battalion had paused in its passage across Eastern Europe, in fact indicative of nothing worse than a legitimate exercise in self-defence? QC Robertson had already suggested that the hangings in Minsk were executions of partisans who had shot at Axis troops – terrible punishment, perhaps, but punishment which would have been meted out by any army.

'In October/November,' continued Donald Robertson, 'the winter of 1941, the activities of the partisans were such that the Germans were very concerned about them, and that is why, or one of the reasons why, they sent the battalions down from Lithuania?'

'There was a certain degree of concern,' conceded the historian. '. . . The Germans, however, put the label of partisan activity on the killing of thousands of people who had no demonstrable connection with partisans at all.'

'[The Lithuanians] were told that they were going to be asked to engage in expelling remnants of the Bolshevik army and Bolshevik partisans?'

'They were certainly told that. Whether they believed it is another matter . . . Some of [them] were acutely aware of the shooting of Jews in Lithuania and perhaps the thought was not far away that they would be doing the same thing in Byelorussia.'

And the other plank of Mr Robertson's case was, of course, the dismissal of evidence from the Soviet Union. 'Have you got a view about Soviet justice in the way that they deal with political cases?' he asked.

'I honestly believe we won't have any difference of opinion about that subject.'

'I take it then you don't have a high opinion of the system of justice in the Soviet Union?'

'No, no. In fact, I have an allergic reaction to it as soon as you mention it.'

Could not the war-crimes documents which the Soviets had made available to Professor Hilberg and others have been carefully selected, suggested Donald Robertson.

'Well, it was not quite as simple as that . . . [Professor Hilberg's investigative group in the Soviet Union] was very experienced, and it was not very easy, to put it bluntly, to pull the wool over our eyes. We knew the manner in which captured records were deposited in archives.'

In other words, and crucially, even when a truth appears from within the belly of a deceitful, despotic state such as the Soviet Union, it is still the truth. It may be smeared by association, but its intrinsic value is intact. Professor Raul Hilberg left the witness stand after two half-days and two full days of questioning, and the defence organised by Peter Watson was grateful for his stamina.

And the other witnesses came on, from Ross Wilson to two police officers testifying that Antanas Gecas had had a stone thrown through his window and had received a bullet in

the post following Scottish Television's programmes. Professor
John Paxton Grant, holder of the Chair in Public International
Law at the University of Glasgow, testified that 'put briefly, a
war crime is a crime committed in time of war by a member of
the armed forces or someone operating under the control or
orders of the armed forces against another person . . . a war
crime is a breach of the laws and customs of war'. Professor
Grant read out to the court Article 6(b) of the Nuremburg
Charter:

> War Crimes, namely violations of the laws or customs of
> war. Such violations shall include, but not be limited to,
> murder, ill-treatment or deportation to slave labour or for any
> other purpose of civilian population of or in occupied territory,
> murder or ill-treatment of prisoners-of-war or persons on the
> seas, killing of hostages, plunder of private or public property,
> wanton destruction of cities, towns or villages, or devastation
> not justified by military necessity.

Professor Grant was asked if, in 1941, there were any
circumstances in which the laws and customs of war permitted
soldiers to kill civilians. He could, he said, think of three:
'Where the civilian was engaged in hostilities himself, was
participating in the fighting, that civilian loses the protection
of the laws of war; where the civilian was threatening a soldier,
which is akin to self-defence; and finally where a civilian is
killed incidentally in a genuine military operation.'
'What is your position,' requested Colin Campbell, 'so far
as guilt is concerned of a person who knowingly participates
in the execution of civilians?'
'As guilty as the principal.'
'And would that extend to whatever form that participation took, if it formed part of the overall operation of the
unlawful killing of civilians?'
'Yes.'

'What about protecting other troops who are in fact carrying out the unlawful execution?'

'Yes.'

Rochelle Picholz, who as 15-year-old Rochelle Weissman had been hidden in a barrel in Slutsk while her people were murdered in the streets outside, arrived from her new home in New York to tell the court of her ordeal.

And on Tuesday, 5 May 1992, Antanas Gecas took the witness stand himself.

'How many times were you in the area of Slutsk?' he was asked by his counsel, Donald Robertson.

'Only once, once . . . past Slutsk.'

'Past Slutsk?'

'Past Slutsk.'

'When was that?'

'1943.'

'Have you ever been actually in the town of Slutsk?'

'No.'

Did he recall being interviewed by Neal Sher in 1982, and requesting the attendance of a British police officer?

'Yes. Didn't want to be trapped by the KGB, because lots of Americans are very communist, could speak American but they were KGB agents.' He had been confused when Sher arrived, he said – 'It was out of the blue, out of nature, working in the pits, in the mines, and then they came . . .'

'Do you remember any occasion when you witnessed a hanging in Minsk?'

'Yes, I remember that. On Sunday got orders to get all battalion and officers had to wear the swords, parade dress . . . When we arrived there Germans came and start hanging people . . .'

'Were you told by anybody why these people were being hanged?'

'No. All what we knew, that they were Bolshevik partisans.'

The next day, the 14th of the hearing, Colin Campbell stepped forward.

'You indicated to us yesterday, I think,' he said, 'that at the time when Mr Sher came to visit you . . . you were perhaps a little confused.'

'Yes.'

'You suggested as a possible reason for that that you had been on night-shift in the pits.'

'That is correct.'

'Yet later in your evidence . . . you told us that you retired from the mines in 1978.'

'1978, correct.'

'So what is puzzling me is how in 1982 you could have been confused because of coming off night-shift in the pit, when you had retired four years previously.'

Gecas was shaken. 'I was confused, completely confused.'

But there was more than confusion in his retraction of earlier statements that he had been in Slutsk in 1941, said Colin Campbell.

'You realised that you had put yourself in the town of Slutsk at the time of the massacre, and as soon as you realised that, you retracted the evidence. That's the simple fact, isn't it? . . . What you are now saying, if I understand you correctly, is that the only occasion when you were anywhere near Slutsk was when you were passing on the Minsk to Brest highway in a military convoy collecting supplies?'

'Yes, in 1943.'

'But in your signed statement [to Neal Sher] what you said was that you remember going to the Slutsk area to fight.'

'Slutsk area? I'm stressed if you call Lanark area "Lanarkshire", it doesn't mean to be in Lanark.'

'We've also heard,' continued Campbell, 'evidence from Mr Aleksynas in this case that he was at Slutsk at the time of the massacre of a large percentage of the Jewish population of Slutsk.'

'He told what KGB told him to say.'

What had Lieutenant Antanas Gecevicius thought he was doing in Byelorussia in 1941? asked Campbell 'You accept that the general pattern of things was that you would go to a village, just putting it fairly generally, somebody would go into the village, collect some people, take them out of the village, and shoot them?'

'We believed they were the Bolsheviks and partisans.'

'Not the Jews?'

'I don't know, maybe they were looking for . . . but I don't know. I can't answer that.'

'Why were children shot?'

'I didn't see any children shot. I didn't see any child or woman shot.'

Slowly, surely, the contradictions woven into Antanas Gecas's various statements and testimony were picked apart and exposed. Finally, admissions were extracted.

'In Byelorussia,' said Colin Campbell, 'in the latter half of 1941 you knew that your battalion was helping to execute innocent people?'

'Yes.'

'Didn't you?'

'No – innocent not. I wouldn't say they were all innocent. Some of them were innocent people but mostly they were the Bolsheviks, communists, the ex-officials.'

Colin Campbell concluded his examintion of Antanas Gecas on the 17th day of the trial. 'The fact is,' he told the pursuer, 'that once you got to Minsk you found yourself engaged in these operations which had nothing to do with fighting Russian soldiers; what they had to do with was killing innocent people – Dukara was an example – and you carried on taking part.'

'I did not take part. I was outside killing area.'

'Even if we were to accept that – which, as you know, I don't – you were there, according to you, in your support unit protecting the people who were carrying out this terrible atrocity.'

'But not shooting.'

'And you carried on doing this on several occasions without as much as a protest to anyone.'

'If you read,' protested Antanas Gecas, 'in any military, in any country's military books, you have not such a thing, you can't protest against – you are court-martialled if you protest against military establishment.'

'So what it comes to is this: you just followed orders.'

'Followed orders,' agreed Antanas Gecas. 'But didn't shoot, didn't kill anybody.'

'I have no further questions,' said Colin Campbell.

On 17 July 1992 Lord James Milligan gave his judgement on the affair of Antanas Gecas. After a full summary of the proceedings, he offered his own opinion:

'I hold it proved on the evidence as a whole,' said Lord Milligan, 'that by the time he moved to Minsk in October 1941 the pursuer was well aware not only of the widespread executions of Jews and other innocent civilians, but of the involvement of members of his Lithuanian Battalion in such executions ... The documentary evidence convincingly excluded any question of a single platoon such as the pursuer's, let alone a whole company such as the pursuer's, not being actively involved in participation in these operations where innocent civilians were methodically killed, often in large numbers. In summary, as platoon commander of a platoon in that battalion throughout that period there was no way in which the pursuer was not actively involved in participation in such operations.'

Juozas Aleksynas, recalled the judge, 'was the first witness to give evidence, but reviewing his evidence in the light of all the other evidence in the case, I have no reason to vary my initial impression of convincing credibility.'

The same did not apply to Aleksynas's former platoon commander. Antanas Gecas, found Lord Milligan, 'was hesitant, guarded, ill-at-ease and not materially consistent on matters which were controversial . . . Far from him telling the truth about his duties in Byelorussia during the last three months of 1941, his evidence, in my assessment, was very far from the truth.

'At best for the pursuer, he attributed to that period duties in which he was involved at later times and, in doing so, denied involvement in horrific events which must be well imprinted in his memory.

'I am satisfied that during that period he participated in many operations in which innocent civilians, and Jews in particular, were killed . . . In particular, I am satisfied that he participated in the operations referred to by Mr Aleksynas in his evidence, including that at Slutsk, an operation in which probably, on the evidence at this proof, a minimum of 5,900 Jewish men, women and children of all ages were murdered and which Mr Simpson properly accepted as comparable qualitatively with mass murder at Auschwitz.'

Turning to his vital conclusion 'as to whether the defenders have proved the truth of the various specific allegations', Lord Milligan ruled:

'The pursuer committed war crimes against Soviet citizens who were old men, women and children. I am clearly satisfied on the evidence as a whole upon the standard of proof agreed to apply to this case that the pursuer participated in many operations involving the killing of innocent Soviet citizens, including Jews in particular, in Byelorussia during the last three months of 1941 . . . It inevitably follows that the pursuer committed war crimes against innocent civilians of all ages and both sexes in the course of these specific operations, it not being in dispute that he was in active command of his platoon throughout the period mentioned . . .

'That the pursuer was Mr Aleksynas's platoon commander throughout the period in question, indeed throughout Mr Aleksynas's seven-month service in Byelorussia, I am fully satisfied. I am also fully satisfied that Mr Aleksynas's platoon was involved in the operations described by him and in particular that the horrendous events in which effectively he was admitting his own involvement did happen and were neither invented by him nor somehow implanted irrevocably in his mind by the KGB.'

The real reason, posited the judge, 'why the Lithuanian Battalion was moved by the German Command from Kaunas to Minsk when it was, was for precisely that use, namely to undertake the actual execution of those to be killed. I further consider it probable that, so far as the German Command was concerned, the Lithuanian Battalion's usefulness to them during the last quarter of 1941, at least, lay virtually wholly, if not wholly, in such duties.'

Judge Milligan found that Scottish Television had not entirely proved that Antanas Gecas 'finished off' victims, adding, 'personally, I am inclined to think that it is rather better than neutral for the defenders in that, on balance, it should properly be regarded as a humane rather than inhumane act in the hideously special circumstances involved.

'In my opinion,' he concluded, 'the defenders succeed in their defence in relation to all the matters averred against them. Accordingly, I hold that the pursuer's case on liability fails . . . I am satisfied that the defender's staff concerned in fact acted in all good faith and in particular believed sincerely in the truth of what they included in the programme.'

Scottish Television had won their case. In the final paradoxical twist, the first war-crimes action to be brought in Great Britain had resulted in defeat for the prosecution. But it was a civil case, and the prosecution represented the alleged war criminal himself. JUDGE BRANDS GECAS MASS MURDERER AND WAR CRIMINAL, the headlines would read on the following day.

Outside Scottish Television a beaming David Scott told all concerned that he had believed all along that the case would be won. 'How do you feel about hounding an old man?' a journalist asked Bob Tomlinson.

He paused, and thought of the old, broken light which

swung over the Ninth Fort at Kaunas, the light which had illuminated those who walked the Path of Death. What victory was there here? 'We have never pursued an old man,' Tomlinson said finally. 'We looked at the conduct of a 24-year-old soldier, who now happens to be an old man.' He thought again. 'I have seen the absolute depravity that can exist in times of war,' he said. 'I am not Jewish and I am not a communist, but that anybody can kill somebody, using either of those things as a reason, is beyond comprehension.'

AFTERWORD

Nineteen months later the non-victory was complete. On Thursday, 3 February 1994 Gavin Ruxton of the Scottish Crown Office War Crimes Unit announced that the unit was to be disbanded, after investigating 17 cases and deciding that in no single case could they mass sufficient evidence to mount a war-crimes prosecution under the stern rigours of Scottish criminal law.

The Crown Office's statement read: 'After careful consideration, Crown counsel have decided that as matters stand there is not at present sufficient evidence for a criminal prosecution in any of the cases reported to them.'

'In some cases,' said Mr Ruxton, 'we managed to uncover contemporary photographs, maps and other documentary evidence in various archives. But the recollection of events by witnesses varied much due to the passage of time. Also, the reaction of some individuals we interviewed who had worked alongside the suspects or had themselves been convicted previously of war crimes, was rather defensive.'

The War Crimes Unit did not deny that it had spent almost £500,000 over three years reaching this conclusion, that it had taken 156 witness statements and followed through over 1,000 inquiries in Germany, Lithuania, Russia, Byelorussia, Israel, Canada, the United States, Australia and New Zealand. But the massively high standard of proof required in a Scottish criminal court, coupled with the fact that such a court could never be expected to travel abroad to accommodate key witnesses outside Scotland, defeated Ruxton and his colleagues.

'We did feel,' he added half-apologetically, 'in relation to some of the allegations that we might be in a position to take things further, but in fact Crown counsel took the decision that there was insufficient evidence to proceed.

'Some of these people,' he said of the 156 witnesses, 'had been convicted of war crimes themselves. They had served beside our suspects. They were less than anxious to tell what they knew. We were struck by how real these events still are for [them].'

At no point in his announcements to the media did Gavin Ruxton mention the name of Antanas Gecas. The headlines in the national press and television news bulletins, however, mentioned hardly anybody else: OUTRAGE AS GECAS ESCAPES PROSECUTION . . . SUSPECTED WAR CRIMINAL WILL NOT BE PROSECUTED . . .

The only possible response, said Ephraim Zuroff in Israel, 'is to express our deepest sense of outrage and indignation. The Bosnian Serbs and all those who have engaged in "ethnic cleansing" will also no doubt breathe a sigh of relief, reinforced by the knowledge that they too will probably never be held accountable for their crimes.'

Merlyn Rees expressed his disappointment, adding that he had hoped for a 'more encouraging decision . . . We note in particular that these files remain active and if further evidence is brought to the attention of the authorities it will be considered.'

But few were in doubt that, while investigations into a further 40 cases were continuing south of the border in England, no resident of Scotland suspected of a crime of war between 1939 and 1945 would thereafter be prosecuted for that crime.

It was not a decision which was welcomed by many. 'Those who survived the atrocities,' editorialised the *Scotsman* newspaper, 'or the families of the victims, are bound to feel that justice for their tormentors has been made ever more elusive.

'. . . These are not matters where rationality is the sole concern. No issue in the twentieth century has been more emotive. There are still millions of people to whom the events of those years are not remote history but raw hurt. A trial that fairly acquits is less inflammatory to such emotions than a trial that never takes place.

'That might seem to veer close to a call for show trials. It is not. On the contrary, we have argued before that standards of proof need to be especially punctilious in relation to events which took place half a century ago, particularly in questions of identification.

'But these are cases in which the old principle holds abundantly true: justice must not only be done, it must be seen to be done. In the case of Mr Gecas, only half at the most of that requirement has been satisfied; and a long dark chapter of history has been left without a proper ending.'

'It's very easy for us,' admitted Gavin Ruxton, 'to say it was all a long time ago, but when you sit by survivors and look into their eyes . . . you can see what it means to them.'